Bill Haley

Bill Haley in his heyday. *Rex Zario Collection*

Bill Haley

The Daddy of Rock and Roll

John Swenson

STEIN AND DAY/*Publishers*/ New York

First published in the United States of America in 1983
Copyright © 1982 by John Swenson
All rights reserved, Stein and Day, Incorporated
Printed in the United States of America
Stein and Day/ *Publishers*
Scarborough House
Briarcliff Manor, N.Y. 10510

Library of Congress Cataloging in Publication Data

Swenson, John.
  Bill Haley, the daddy of rock and roll.

  Discography: p.
  Includes index.
  1. Haley, Bill. 2. Rock musicians—United States—
Biography.
ML420.H1165S9 1983   784.5'4'00924 [B]   82-42760
ISBN 0-8128-2909-3
ISBN 0-8128-6177-9 (pbk.)

Contents

Introduction and Acknowledgements 7
One: And Never Brought To Mind . . . 12
Two: Chester, Pennsylvania 15
Three: Keep Smiling 20
Four: The Saddlemen 24
Five: Rock the Joint 32
Six: Change Is Now 40
Seven: The Sun Never Shines In Studio A 46
Eight: The Golden Age of Rock & Roll 56
Nine: Calling All Comets 61
Ten: Rock & Roll Gets the Blame 69
Eleven: Rocking Around the World 80
Twelve: The Second Battle of Waterloo 86
Thirteen: The Well Runs Dry 104
Fourteen: The Con Man's Con Man 111
Fifteen: The Germans 119
Sixteen: End of An Era 125
Seventeen: The Twist King 131
Eighteen: Rock & Roll Revival 136
Nineteen: Rock Around the Country 140
Twenty: The End 150
Twenty-One: Crazy Man, Crazy 155
Epilogue 162
Discography 165
Index 171

Illustrations

Bill Haley in his heyday   *Frontispiece*
Bill Haley and the Saddlemen   *pg. 28*
Between pp 39 and 40
Labels of early records by Haley and the Saddlemen
Kent Theatre handbill
Between pp 64 and 65
A 1950 sheet music cover picturing Haley
The Four Aces of Western Swing performing
Haley's Four Aces of Western Swing promoting a record
Yodeling Bill Haley
The first rock and roll riot
Bill Haley and the Comets
Haley at the beach
Ralph Jones and Bill Haley
Haley during a Decca recording session
Haley and the Comets on the set of *Don't Knock the Rock*
Between pp 128 and 129
Haley and Jack Howard
Rudy Pompilli
Bill Haley and the Comets
Ralph Jones and Haley
Haley's arrival in England in 1957
Welcoming "the Rock and Roll King"
Haley in 1968, "the Rock 'n' Roll King Forever"
Haley with a 78 rpm record of "Rock Around the Clock"
Haley demonstrates dance steps
Haley in London in 1974
Haley during overseas tour

Rock and roll revival newsclips   *pg 149*
Bill Haley's death certificate   *pg 164*
Newspaper article about Haley's death   *facing pg 164*

Introduction and Acknowledgements

A LOT OF people think Bill Haley was a fluke. The popular mis-
conception, hardened after years of historical acceptance, is that
Haley was a one-hit wonder who stumbled onto 'Rock Around
the Clock' and never accomplished anything beyond that. The
critically orthodox argument goes that Haley was a 'safe' con-
struct of the record business created to capitalise on black
music.

Such judgements of Haley's nature have created a funda-
mental misunderstanding about the very beginnings of rock &
roll. This blind turn in rock history was the fascinating terrain I
travelled through in preparing this book – some of my findings
astonished me, and I'd be surprised if they didn't also illuminate
certain hidden corners of your own ideas about this music.

Haley claimed to have discovered rock & roll, a claim that
was never taken seriously by the time rock history was being
codified in the late '60s. It was dutifully noted that rock & roll
'began' in 1955 with 'Rock Around the Clock' and the film
Blackboard Jungle, but then, the story goes, Haley was quickly
made obsolete by Elvis Presley.

However, when you consider that Haley had been making
rock & roll records since 1951, and playing to audiences of
teenagers several years before the phenomenon is generally considered to have started, his claim to have discovered the music
doesn't seem at all preposterous

In fact Haley established many of the conventions of rock &
roll recording and performance that are still used regularly, with
no thought of their origin, today. His band, the Comets, was far
in advance of any of its contemporaries, and many of their
techniques and strategies anticipated musical developments that
would not resurface for decades. Haley's era was dominated by

dynamic solo personalities, but his absolute emphasis on the importance of his band's sound rather than his own persona clearly sets him apart from the times. Elvis was backed by great musicians, and Buddy Holly recorded without the Crickets with great reluctance, but the Comets were the first real rock & roll *band*, and it wasn't until the Beatles developed the band concept on its own later that this approach became standard practice. Haley himself may cut an unimposing figure next to Elvis Presley, but as a bandleader, and as a medium for the music and the audience to discover each other, he was unquestionably a master.

What's more, Haley championed rock & roll all through his life, even when he didn't really understand what it had become. When Presley turned his back on rock & roll to pursue a career as a romantic lead in Hollywood and a post-Sinatra crooner, Haley and the Comets were still earnestly turning out big beat dance music for rock & roll fans.

Assembling the information for this project required arduous research of secondary materials scattered around the globe and tricky primary research to uncover facts about the life of a man whose privacy was extremely well guarded during his career. The task would not have been accomplished without the tireless diligence of Sharon Gude who collected newsclips, hunted down false leads and travelled up and down the eastern seaboard of the United States with me in search of interviews with people who knew Haley.

For much of the time our search seemed futile, but a few key people provided invaluable assistance in directing us where to look. Ed Gruenger of the Chester musicians' union was extremely helpful, as was Dave Shanzer of the Booth Corners Auction Mart, who spent an evening introducing us to a number of people who knew Bill Haley as a child. One of the more remarkable things we discovered in the process was Haley's personal diary from 1957, which had been left behind in a closet of his house. The Kettericks, current owners of Melody Manor, graciously showed us around the place and, in a profound moment, I raised a toast to Bill Haley's spirit at the very basement bar where he stood during his glory days.

Several interviews were conducted by Sharon, myself, and our excellent colleague George Arthur, whose fascination with the subject matter proved to be an invaluable aid at a number of points. We travelled to North Philadelphia to interview the larger than life figure of James E. Myers, publisher of 'Rock Around the Clock' and a number of other Haley sides, in the basement office of the house where he lives with his mother. The room is a monument to 'Rock Around the Clock' itself (the walls are ringed with over 100 different versions of the song) and to Myers' acting career (there are numerous pictures of him posing with Hollywood stars).

We also visited the more modest home of another publisher, Rex Zario, who put his fantastic archives of Haley-ana at our disposal. We conducted an enjoyable interview with former Comets drummer Ralph Jones, an extremely merry man who remembered Haley fondly and showed us home movies of the Comets on the road, in the studio, and relaxing on Haley's yacht. Former Comets Al Rex and Frank Beecher were also very cooperative and patient in answering our numerous phone calls for information.

Sharon and I had a particularly moving encounter with Ann Pompilli, a brave woman who has overcome the heartbreaking death of her husband Rudy, the bulwark of the Comets. Ann took us to the Nite Cap lounge, where virtually everyone in the place recalled Rudy's performances.

Some of our journeys were fascinating glimpses into the past. I'll never forget the first time we drove into Chester, past the bleak miles of factories, shipyards and smokestacks belching acrid smoke that seemed to permeate every corner of the city. The town itself has been left for dead – the old building where Haley's office once was is now part of a poverty stricken, crumbling slum neighbourhood.

In order to talk to Kenny Roberts, who taught Haley some of his yodelling techniques and still travels under the motto 'the world's greatest yodeller,' we had to go to a country and western bar called Rainbow's End in Woodridge, New Jersey. Rainbow's End overlooks the New Jersey meadowlands. It's a spacious room with a stage against the wall in the center and a circular bar immediately in front of the stage, surrounded on three sides by tables. When we arrived a young country rock band was playing songs by Eddie Rabbit and Waylon Jennings to an oblivious audience.

9

Kenny Roberts walked in and the atmosphere suddenly shifted completely. A tall, imposing figure in a fire-engine red cowboy suit and ten gallon stetson, Roberts took the stage and began reeling off one astonishing yodel after another. The guitarist of the country rock band, which was backing Roberts, stared at him in disbelief as he played. The crowd suddenly exploded into life, whooping and cheering Roberts on after each yodelling sequence. It was easy to understand the point Roberts made later in my interview: 'Bill should have thrown a few yodels into his rock & roll act at the end. That would really have gotten them going.'

Probably the most poignant moment in the research for this book came when we met Haley's eldest son Jack, who lives with his wife Patty and their daughter Jacqueline in a small house in Salem, New Jersey, the town where Haley first met Dorothy Crowe and lived during that first marriage. Prominently displayed on Jack's living room walls are two paintings-on-velvet, facing each other. One is of Elvis Presley; the other, of Bill Haley.

Jack has been crusading to revive interest in his father's music. A letter written by Jack to Dick Clark prompted Clark to reconsider Haley's position in the 25th anniversary American Bandstand show, which featured a climactic finale of 'Rock Around the Clock.'

Finally, special thanks must go to Ken Terry, a good reporter who had been on the trail of a Haley story in 1979, and managed the remarkable feat of tracking the elusive Haley down and getting him to agree to an in-depth interview – a considerable achievement because Haley refused to talk to the press during his last years. It's a measure of the depth of feeling against Haley that despite Terry's accumulation of some sensational material the story was turned down by a number of publications, including the *Village Voice,* because Haley wasn't deemed a fit subject for scrutiny. To Terry, and to Haley's producers, Milt Gabler and Sam Charters, who both provided splendid overviews of the man's career, I am indeed indebted.

Thanks also to the host of others who helped the project along in a variety of different ways: Dan Doyle, Barbara Mathe, Gilbert and Jane Gude, Justin Pearson, Tony DeMeur, John Morthland, Nick Tosches, Bix Reichner, Jim Feddis, Michael

Neve, Keith Erskine, Mike Bailey, Edward Swenson, Reg Venters, Dennis Mahoney, Gareth Hawksworth, Bruce Olsen, Rob Hunter, John Alexander, Dorothy Crowe, Lynn Kellerman, Geoff Thorn, Dot and Wilfred Davis, Clem Taylor, Sgt. Charley Griffen, M and Co., Sheri Safran, Glenn Cowley, Paul Cooper, Arti Kunst, Rounder Records, Harvey Smith and Shorty Cook.

Bill Haley

One: And Never Brought To Mind . . .

DAWN BROKE BLEAKLY on the torn streets of Chester, Pennsylvania. The squat two and three story brick houses that had sheltered this city's generations of immigrants were blasted by the fierce east wind as it drove across the Delaware River out over New Jersey and toward the wintery Atlantic.

It was Tuesday morning, 5th February, in the year of America's Bicentennial celebration, 1976. Three sleek black Lincoln Continental limousines purred discreetly at the curb outside the Church of St. Anthony of Padua, the social focal point of the area's large Italian-American community. As the muted sounds of mourning swelled out from the church doors, the early morning funeral procession gathered for its final duty.

Harsh winter light bleached all life from the scene, giving the procession the curious aspect of an old black and white movie as the limousines, hearse and dozens of cars in the motorcade flashed on their high beams and slowly began their formation drive, winding through the streets of Chester on the twenty minute journey to St. Peter and Paul's Cemetery in Broomall. There the bystanders gathered around the open grave where the celebrant, vested in the black cope used in the Masses for the Dead, prepared Rudy Pompilli's body for burial.

'Let us pray', said the priest as he prepared to bless the grave. 'Oh God, by Whose mercy rest is given to the souls of the faithful, in Your kindness bless this grave . . .' The crowd, which included the most respected members of the Chester musicians' union and several members of Bill Haley's Comets, the band Rudy had played in for the last twenty years of his life, watched the priest sprinkle holy water and incense onto the coffin and the grave.

'I am the resurrection,' said the priest. 'Blessed be the Lord,

12

the God of Israel, because He has visited and wrought redemption for His people, and has raised up a horn of salvation for us . . .'

Annie Pompilli, the tough Scottish woman who had married Rudy only two months previously when both she and her husband knew he was close to death from lung cancer, had prepared for this moment but could not stop her tears. Rudy's saxophone meant so much to him – only a week before he had played in public despite his intense pain, and he had told her he wanted to die with the horn in his mouth. For Rudy, 'a horn of salvation' was most appropriate.

The priest took his leave. Rudy Pompilli was buried. The mourners, numbed with the cold and their love for Rudy, slowly resumed their own lives as they carried out Rudy's last request. A dixieland quartet led by Ed Gruenger, president of the Chester musicians' union, set up by the graveside and began to play the three songs Rudy wanted his friends to hear at his burial. The wind stung their faces and threatened to topple Gruenger's drums as they played 'People,' which had been Rudy and Ann's wedding theme a few months earlier.

When the band played the traditional New Orleans funeral march, 'When the Saints Go Marching In', tears and smiles mixed as the people remembered the tune as Rudy's trademark. Twenty years before his merry saxophone had interpreted the tune with the Comets as 'Saints Rock & Roll', and the song had become Rudy's trademark at the Nite Cap, the local club where he played under the name of Rudy Pell fronting a band called the Happy Days.

At the Nite Cap 'When the Saints Go Marching In' was the showstopper. Rudy would march off the stage, playing his saxophone, cross the club and climb onto the bar, blowing furiously as he arch-stepped down the bar, never spilling a drink, then jumped to the floor and started a snake dance with more and more of the crowd following him while he played and marched into the ladies' room, into the men's room, came out with a toilet paper rol that he flung across the club, out of the club and into the parking lot . . . Rudy's friends loved to watch him play 'When the Saints Go Marching In' and they followed him, for the last time, right up until he was covered with six feet of earth.

Somewhere in Mexico, Bill Haley shuddered and took another

drink of scotch. Haley knew Rudy Pompilli's death meant the bitter end of his fifteen-year-old comeback dream. Haley never really accepted the fact that his greatest days had passed. He'd failed time after time to recapture the hit single formula that had made him the King of Rock & Roll in 1955 with 'Rock Around the Clock'. One by one, when times were bad, the band he had broken attendance records with around the world left him, but Rudy had stuck with him. Year after year Rudy faithfully put together another unit of Comets to record or tour with Haley. With Rudy gone Haley was left all to himself.

It was a measure of how badly things had turned out for Haley that he felt unable to attend the funeral of his best friend, a guy he constantly referred to as his brother. There were unpleasant memories waiting for him back in Chester, Pennsylvania, where he had once been on top of the world. These included two ex-wives, a number of people he couldn't trust, friends he was too embarrassed to see in his failure, and a list of disgruntled creditors. All in all Chester was a place where Haley was reluctant to show his face. Before Rudy's death, Haley would slip into town from time to time to stay with his friend. Now that too was at an end.

Two: Chester, Pennsylvania

WILLIAM HALEY WAS born in Highland Park, Michigan, on July 6, 1925. His father, William Haley senior, had moved to the Detroit area from Kentucky to find work in the thriving industrial community there. His mother, Maude Green, was the daughter of a baker in Ulverston, England. She had come to the States during her teens.

In 1928 Herbert Hoover was elected president of the United States. Prosperity was still the keynote in the country's industrial areas, but a growing agricultural slump cast an ominous shadow over the future. The stock market crash of 1929 brought economic ruin to the large numbers of middle class people who'd invested in the market and triggered the Great Depression of the '30s. Hoover and his economic advisers apparently miscalculated the severity of the national collapse, and soon factories were closing everywhere. By the early '30s a full twenty-five per cent of the population was unemployed.

Detroit and the surrounding area was devastated. William Haley Sr. took his wife and their two children (Bill and his younger sister, Margaret) and, like a lot of other Americans, went looking for work. Wisely, Haley headed east instead of west, and settled in the hills of Boothwyn, Pennsylvania, a few miles away from the Delaware River valley town of Chester. Here Haley found employment in the Sun shipyards.

William Haley was fortunate to have a job during those bleak economic times. His family enjoyed a marginally higher standard of living than the impoverished farmers in his neighbourhood. Haley was able to afford a late model car and his son Bill was treated to a bicycle, an almost unheard-of luxury that made him the envy of his friends at school. Huett Davis, who still lives in Boothwyn opposite the house where Haley lived as a

15

child, remembers Bill as being better off than his schoolmates.

'His father had a job, you see,' Davis explains. 'At that time I didn't have a father, my father was dead and we were in poverty you might say. My mother was trying to raise a bunch of kids and we always thought he had quite a bit – he had a bicycle.'

There was an open field near the Davis house where the local kids would get together to play baseball, and Bill used to join in the fun. 'His father had a cigarette-making machine,' Davis recalls. 'And he'd get his father's tobacco and paper and he'd make cigarettes for us and bring it down to our place, and we'd go down to the creek and smoke and swim, so that's how we liked Bill Haley. We always waited for Bill to come down and bring us cigarettes. We were kids and we were all about on the same level as far as what we had and did and we were all poor and we didn't realize it. At that time everybody was poor around the community here, everybody had the same thing and it wasn't too much, but we all enjoyed it, whatever it was. Once in a while we'd get enough pennies together and get Marlboro cigarettes for ten cents a pack and boy, they were really great.

Sgt. Charley Griffen, a lifelong resident of the area who is a security guard at the auction mart at Booth Corners to this day, recalls Haley well. 'We all went to the one-room schoolhouse at Booth Corners,' he says. 'Six grades in the room, and one teacher.' They used to tab the place with the quaint slogan 'Corn cob college, where you get your knowledge.'

'I used to steal Bill Haley's bicycle,' Griffen remembers, shaking his head. 'We didn't like the girls at our school, we liked the girls up at the other school, so we'd steal Bill's bike and go up there. He didn't like that at all. I was the school bully.'

But Huett Davis remembers Bill as being easygoing about his bike. 'Like I say he'd come down and play ball and go swimming and fish and clown around – he always had a bicycle. Us boys loved to ride his bicycle. He was good-hearted, you know, when he was a kid like that, he'd let you ride his bike.'

Sometimes the local kids would try to raise money for their baseball team or some other social function by putting on a show. The fire house would be the site of minstrel shows and variety shows for which the kids would charge twenty-five cents admission. Bill was invited to play at the shows, which were probably his first public appearances. 'Haley used to bring his guitar to school with him,' Griffen recalled. 'He'd play it after school sometimes.'

Huett Davis helped put on those shows, and remembered Haley's participation. 'He was just one of the boys in the act. He put on his own deal. It was like a talent show, more or less, that's what it really amounted to. He was playing country music then. I remember real well one of the songs he sang was "Chime bells are ringing, Yodel-ay-dee-hoo." That must have been '37, '38, in that neighborhood.'

Haley had been surrounded by music at home. His father played banjo and his mother was a technically accomplished keyboardist with classical training. She occasionally taught piano and is said to have played the organ at the Baptist Church in nearby Marcus Hook. In later years Haley would tell the story that he was so fascinated by the music he heard around the house that he went and fashioned a simulated guitar out of cardboard and his parents were so moved that they went out and got him a real one.

Gene Autry was the most famous of the 'singing cowboys' that came to popularity around this time. Autry serials at the Marcus Hook theater on a Saturday afternoon fired Bill's fantasy to become a musician. He had a good ear and learned to fashion chords by trial and error after hearing songs on the radio. He also taught himself to yodel, and though he mostly kept his music to himself, Haley slowly became popular in the neighborhood for his playing and singing. 'He was a little on the quiet side,' Huett Davis says.

Haley's shyness came from the fact that he had been blind in the left eye since infancy, the result of a crudely performed mastoid operation by a local doctor. Haley was self-conscious about his appearance, and strove hard to hide his affliction after he became successful by carefully arranging his pose on all official photographs – which is why his press photos often make him out to look so inanimate. Haley never told people of this affliction, and his reticence added a poignant twist to his attempts to befriend the local kids. But it also made him an outsider, and a target for abuse.

'I know he had a bad eye,' says Davis, 'and I think that had a big part in his shyness. I know at times us kids would make fun of him that way, you know, and he'd want to fight about it. One

17

time we were playing ball and it came out, something about the eye anyhow, and there was a fight right then and there so I'm sure he was self-conscious about it.'

Down the road from Bill Haley's house was the Booth Corners auction mart, the center of all social activity in the area each weekend. It was a farmer's market made up out of three old barns that had been connected together. Chickens scurried around among the farmers as salesmen hawked virtually everything a farmer might need from livestock to tractor parts – as well as a lot of things nobody needed, like snake oil. On one side of the barns was a medicine show, and on the other side there was live music. There was a guy named Ed McMahon selling vegetable choppers, but what he really wanted was to be in show business.

Young Bill hung out at the auction mart, sweeping up and doing odd jobs, and one day the manager asked him to play his guitar for him in his office. 'I was too shy to play in public,' Haley later recalled. 'He asked me to sing for his big audience – but I never figured I'd have the nerve. What I didn't know is that he had secretly rigged a microphone in his office and some loud-speakers in the mart. So I had my first audience before I knew about it. And they seemed to like it all right. So I went on doing it – out in front of the public – for a dollar a night.'

Auction Mart manager Dave Shanzer remembers Haley well. 'Bill used to hang around the sale, he used to clean up, he loved it. He'd sweep, he'd help Bill Ormsby, who was our maintenance man at the time. There used to be a saying "What are you doing Friday night? Meet you at the sale." It was either here or at the firehouse.

'We had a midway here. Right outside my office was this big oak tree and we used to have two fruit tables pushed together. We'd have a string of lights up there over the stage. Bill used to come over on Friday nights. He'd come with his straw cowboy hat on and his cowboy boots and play this hillbilly music. People would stand around and watch him and he'd play for half an hour. They loved him. A fella by the name of Slim Calucci used to pay him, then I was paying him two dollars. They liked him so much around here, though, that we ended up paying him five dollars, which was a lot of money back then.

'His father used to come down and watch him,' Shanzer

18

added. 'Everybody came, really, this was the center of all social activity. We had a medicine man, the Mighty Adam, he sold snake oil that he made himself. We had the Indian man come out and do tricks with rattlesnakes. One guy, he would take horseshoes and pull them apart, he would pull a car with ten or twelve people on it by his hair. People used to come out to watch all this, it didn't cost them anything. They were pitching medicine, snake oil, there were guys pitching wax for the cars. Bill Ormsby would have the knock-the-milk-bottles-down games. It was all country atmosphere. When Bill Haley got through, the auctioneer would get up and start auctioning off on the tables. He'd auction off boxes of eggs and bananas by the stalk.'

At first Haley played alone, but later he was joined by another guitarist, Ray McCann. Dot Davis, a local girl who would occasionally join in on accordion, remembers Haley playing 'Has Anybody Seen My Gal'.

Once Haley started performing he never stopped, but he kept his aspirations mostly to himself. 'I never heard him saying to me or anybody else about going big time with it,' says Huett Davis. But with no discouragement from his music-loving parents, and the only alternative a future at the Viscose factory, it's easy to see how Haley might have decided to make his living as a musician.

At that time there were small amusement parks dotting the Pennsylvania, New Jersey and Delaware area, and these parks would feature live entertainment, mostly country artists. Haley found work there at places like Sunset Park and Rainbow Park around his hometown before signing on with local celebrity Cousin Lee's band.

Cousin Lee had a popular syndicated radio show based out of Wilmington, Delaware, and eventually he became so successful that he formed his own park in the Wilmington area, which featured his own bands and Nashville artists like Patsy Cline and Hankshaw Hawkins. Haley sang and played guitar with the Cousin Lee band. He built up a small following and started to improve his singing and yodelling to the point where he could start thinking about going out on his own.

19

Three: Keep Smiling

WORLD WAR II meant good times for Lee Park. Cousin Lee and his wife Sarah were the toast of Delaware. Their show on WDEL in Wilmington was an institution that generated so much business for their mail order songbooks that a secretary had to be hired to keep track of the correspondence. The park featured musical performances from a band that ranged from three to a dozen members, though the usual number was eight. In addition to the music, rides and amusements brought in the public, and the Lees got a chance to showcase custom western wear like their matching V for Victory cowboy outfits with the wartime good luck charm emblazoned on the arms. Publisher Jack Howard, who would later produce some of Haley's earliest recordings, ran a novelty shop on the premises. One of Howard's songs, 'Keep Smiling,' was used as Cousin Lee's theme, and Haley would often sing the tune at the park:

> When everything goes wrong keep smiling
> When everything goes wrong just laugh
> Throw back your shoulder stick up your chin
> Long as you can smile you're bound to win

Considering what would happen to Haley over the years these seem particularly ironic lyrics.

Haley played with Lee's band at a number of local dances in addition to the park appearances and radio shows. In an antique southern New Jersey town called Salem, Lee's band played the Parish town center, and there Lee's young singing cowboy met a ravishing local girl, Dorothy Crowe.

Bill and Dorothy started to go out together and the young singer told his sweetheart about his ambition to make it to the big time. He was going nowhere with Cousin Lee and figured he had to get out of the area. His first break came in the form of an advertisement in the music trade magazine *Billboard* for a singing yodeller to replace Kenny Roberts in the Downhomers, one of the most popular bands in the midwest.

The Downhomers were led by Shorty Cook and were based at that time out of station WOWO in Fort Wayne, Indiana, where they played a daily show and hosted the extremely popular Saturday night barn dance, the Hoosier Hop. Their hot young yodeller, Kenny Roberts, turned eighteen in late 1944 and was immediately drafted. Yodelling cowboys were at a premium, and Haley's blind eye kept him out of the draft. 'He came right here and I hired him on the spot,' recalls Cook. 'They was grabbin' 'em all up for the war. Everybody that was available, they grabbed him up.'

Haley had only about a week to learn Roberts' parts but the two young yodellers, who were about the same age, got along well. 'He was a nice kid,' says Roberts. 'He was a little nervous but that was understandable because the Downhomers were probably his first big group.'

Both Haley and Roberts were disciples of the great yodeller Elton Britt, but Roberts was the more advanced of the two and taught Haley several of his trick yodels, the fast falsetto voice breaks and rolling octaves. 'I sang the high tenor,' Roberts later pointed out, 'and the high harmony parts on the western trios, so he had to learn those. He had to learn to play the bass fiddle like I did too.'

Haley got his parts down fast. 'He was very good,' says Roberts. 'When I left he was coming along real good. He turned out to be a damn good yodeller.'

Cook also remembers being impressed with Haley's technique. 'He was an extremely good yodeller.' Cook noted that Haley also had an excellent ear. 'His main asset was that he could hear something on the radio and remember the words and the tune, which none of the rest of us could do.' But Cook never expected Haley to go on to bigger things. 'He was probably the least likely to succeed of the whole bunch,' laughs Cook. 'But you never know. He didn't have that much push about him, but he hit on the right thing.'

According to Cook, Haley had talked about making crossover records even back then. 'We talked about a lot of that

21

stuff long before he ever left us, about combining country music with pop music so they would get both fields. I wrote a lot of songs with him but nothing that was rock & roll at that time. He was gone before the rock & roll era came in, so I never wrote any rock & roll for him. We never recorded any of them. One of them was "Four Leaf Clover Blues," we still have the sheet music to that. But it never amounted to a hill of beans.'

Cook's memories of Haley are not particularly pleasant because, after a salary dispute, Bill left in 1946 along with several other members of the band. 'He jumped the show with Bob Mason and Lloyd Cornell,' Cook explains. 'They came up Saturday night and said "We're jumping the show, we'll see you later." They wanted to start on their own and make a million dollars. They wanted to all get rich. I told Haley before he left he was going to be sorry because that was a pretty bad pair he left with, especially that Mason. He'd done this to other bands, he'd take them with him and get going good somewhere and he'd move them out so he'd be the whole boss. See they left as a trio and picked up a couple of other guys and they were all three going to be bosses, but it wasn't long until Haley got booted out.'

Cook claims that Haley subsequently tried to rejoin the Downhomers. 'He knocked at the door at about three o'clock in the morning. I had to get out of bed and come down and let him in. He was broke so I gave him about forty or fifty bucks. That's when he went back to Chester.'

Whether or not this story is entirely accurate, Haley later admitted he returned home disillusioned. 'I busked around the country riding freight trains,' he said in an unpublished interview with investigative reporter Ken Terry two years before his death, 'the usual story, playing in radio stations and what have you. I did a stint in Chicago at the International Barn Dance, and played in St Louis and Dallas, Louisiana and out through the midwest. Then I returned home. My mom and dad were living near Philadelphia and I returned there with disillusion at the grand old age of twenty two. I had had what I felt was a halfway decent career, but I felt I wasn't going to make it, and I returned with the idea of getting out of show business. Then I became a disc jockey on a local station, WPWA in Chester, because it was in me, but I was still singing country and western.'

22

Haley married Dorothy Crowe upon leaving the Down-homers, when the strikingly beautiful, part American Indian girl joined him in Brattleborough, Vermont. The newlyweds lived in Keane, New Hampshire, then later in Lebanon, Pennsylvania, before returning to Chester. 'We lived up in Chester, right across from the B & O railroad station,' Dorothy later said.

Those postwar years were lean, but Haley had big ideas. 'We had rough times, but they were good times, I think,' recalls Dorothy. 'I can remember living on bread and peanut butter and black coffee just to keep things going. He had that goal, from the day I met him, he was going to get to the top one way or another. That's one thing I always respect him for – he got there. Because I had so many friends in this town who used to make fun of him and laugh at him you know, before he got to the top. When he got there then they bragged about knowing him.'

Dorothy was another one of the people who knew Haley before his success and recalls the curious fact of his shyness. 'I tell people and they look at me like I'm crazy,' she says, 'but Bill was a very shy person. He hated to go into a new place and meet new people, and for someone in that business, it seemed so strange. But I can remember the boys begging him to come out of the dressing room when people wanted to meet him, they would have to almost force him out. Once he got mingling with people it was all right, but it was that first step, it was very hard for him.'

Four: The Saddlemen

THE YEARS FOLLOWING World War II saw hillbilly music move from its original roots in the South-eastern United States to one of the country's most popular forms. Jack Howard was a tireless promoter of country and western music in the Philadelphia area. In fact Howard was a crucial figure in breaking down the myth that country and western was a peculiarly Southern medium by introducing the great Canadian c & w star Hank Snow to the U.S. Howard was extremely proud of his photo scrap-book which posed him with such c & w stars as Gene Autry and Roy Rogers.

Cowboy Records, the small independent label started by Howard, was Philadelphia's first record company. It marked the beginning of an auspicious music-making history in a city that would subsequently become a music industry center. In 1946, when Howard started the company, the music world was in the process of considerable change, and a number of forward-looking performers and entrepreneurs recognized this as their big chance. Up until 1940 all music in the United States was published by a single organization, the American Society of Composers, Authors and Publishers (ASCAP). ASCAP was interested almost exclusively in the song factory products of New York's famed tin pan alley while completely ignoring the popular regional styles of blues, hillbilly and cowboy music which, as a result, was almost never heard in the lucrative northern markets.

In 1940 ASCAP made a terrible miscalculation when the company decided to bludgeon radio stations by declaring a strike if radio didn't double the royalty rate paid for the broadcasting of their material. ASCAP banned the use of all of their songs and radio responded by forming their own organization,

Broadcast Music Industry (BMI). Blues and hillbilly music became BMI's biggest interests, and for the first time radio opened up on a large scale to these performers. BMI would later help to sponsor and promote rock & roll for similar reasons.

So the magic word was 'crossover', which meant making a hillbilly or blues record with a clever enough hook to crack the national pop market. All an aspiring young musician had to do was come up with the right idea. Haley burned with the desire to be the one to do it.

From his base at WPWA Haley plotted his career. By day he'd sing on the air, pitch commercials for local merchants and fill in wherever he could. His first band, the Four Aces of Western Swing, consisted of accordionist Al Constantine, bassist Barney Barnard and guitarist Tex King.

In 1947 Dorothy gave birth to the Haley's first child, Sharyn Anne. Bill wrote a song about his daughter, 'Rose of My Heart', as well as a few other tunes, but when he started to think about recording he decided to cover versions of popular songs by established country and western performers. Haley had known Jack Howard from his days with Cousin Lee, so it was natural for him to approach Howard when he wanted to make records. To record for Cowboy the artist had to pay Howard for the recording and pressing costs – any profit would likely come from selling the records at live performances, but mainly they were promotional tools to further the group's name and make them a more attractive booking prospect.

In 1948 Haley released his first records on Cowboy with the Four Aces of Western Swing. Hank Williams' 'Too Many Parties, Too Many Pals' was the first, backed by 'Four Leaf Clover Blues'. The second release was a cover of George Morgan's 'Candy Kisses', with Red Foley's 'Tennessee Border' on the flip side. Haley's third recording for Cowboy was as a featured vocalist with Reno Browne and her Buckaroos, 'My Sweet Little Girl From Nevada'. Browne was a local television cowgirl star who also made B-movie horse operas for Monogram pictures.

To cut down on expenses Haley recorded his tunes right in the studio at WPWA. Haley had so many different angles going at the station that he practically lived there. He acted as part-time janitor, record librarian, announcer, newscaster, he hosted a 'Ladies Aids' program, played solo, hosted two shows a day with the Four Aces of Western Swing, and sometimes played duets with guitarist Tex King.

Haley's first national press exposure came from his idea to perform a marathon fund-raising program for cancer research. On 16th April 1949, from 6 a.m. to 6.45 p.m., when the station went off the air, Haley and the Four Aces of Western Swing (with Rusty Keefer in place of Tex King) hosted what was billed as 'The first hillbilly and Western marathon'. Other regional radio station personalities showed up – Shorty Long and his Santa Fe Rangers from WEEU in Reading; Jesse and Sally Rogers, the Sleepy Hollow Ranch Gang, Pee Wee Miller, the Murray Sisters, Monte Rosci and Jack Day from WFIL in Philadelphia; and the 101 Ranch Boys from WSBA in York, Pennsylvania. The benefit was a huge success, collecting $16,000.

Around the same time the Four Aces of Western Swing recorded 'Stand Up and Be Counted' and 'Loveless Blues' for Center Records. Shortly afterwards Haley disbanded that group and assembled a dramatically improved band made up of Billy Williamson on steel guitar, John Grande on piano and accordion and Al Rex on bass. People referred to Haley's outfit in abbreviated form as the Four Aces, but there was a popular vocal group from the same area called the Four Aces, so to avoid confusion Haley changed the band's name to the Saddlemen.

The Saddlemen were the nucleus for Haley's rock & roll groups. Haley agreed to make the four of them equal partners in any future success they would have, and he was convinced they'd make it big even then.

Al Rex, whose real name is Al Piccarelli, recalls that the other group members, who all held day jobs in addition to their work as the Saddlemen, didn't share Haley's optimism. 'He had a little office down in the basement at the radio station and he had all these wild dreams. He'd say "When we make it big we're going to have our own publishing company, we're going to have our own record company." I used to say to myself "This son-of-a-bitch is crazy you know, he's crazy!" '

However, the four made some great recordings together, many of which were never released. 'Yodel Your Blues Away', a song written by Haley and Jack Howard, wasn't released until an Australian record company put it out in 1977. The song is fantastic, easily as good as much of Haley's better known rock material, and shows that he had real promise as a country singer. You can also hear the hints of the pre-rock style his band was developing. Though the tune is related to the eastern European polka style popular in the region (local radio still carries a number of polka shows), the driving cadence and rhythm accompaniment is definitely harder edged. Grande's accordion flies through the arrangement at breakneck speed while Haley's expert yodelling twists around in an exciting rush, pushed along by Rex's revolutionary bass playing, which is crudely percussive rather than medolic.

Similarly, the Saddlemen performed a version of 'The Covered Wagon Rolled Right Along' with such spirit that you can hear the basic rhythmic ideas they would later use on their rock material.

'Rovin' Eyes' shows the band's western swing influence, especially via Bob Wills and his Texas Playboys, to good effect. Billy Williamson's lap guitar solo on this tune is tremendous. Haley handles cornpone ballad vocals like 'Within This Broken Heart of Mine' and 'My Mom Heard Me Crying' with the sophistication of a veteran cowboy balladeer, and his reading of Roy Acuff's classic 'Wreck On the Highway' is stirring in its dramatic intensity.

Haley's credentials as a yodeller are well established by 'Yodel Your Blues Away' and Slim Stuart's 'A Yodeller's Lullaby', while 'Foolish Questions' and 'Behind the Eight Ball' show his ability to sing humorous material as well. Haley's idea was to use the cowboy base to cross over to a wider audience. The Saddlemen promoted themselves as 'The most versatile band in the land', and 'The Cowboy Jive Band', describing their music as 'Jive, Cowboy, Popular and Hillbilly'. Even though, back then, the ten-gallon stetson covered Haley's trademark kiss curl ('He'd had it from the day I met him,' says Dorothy) the seeds of the country/blues/pop fusion that would make him a star were already sown.

Haley and the Saddlemen played a variety of dates booked by Howard in the Philadelphia area, everything from ranch parties and picnics to political club functions. The money was never

27

great – they'd get anything from $25 to $200 plus the chance to sell their records. Howard got a small retainer amounting to only five or ten dollars a week. Haley and Howard also had a duo act on Cowboy Stage Shows in Philadelphia theaters. The Saturday afternoon matinee would feature cartoons, a couple of westerns, and Haley and Howard in a comedy act in which Haley would play the straight man, with Howard interrupting him with slapstick routines while he tried to sing his songs.

Howard shared office space with another local publisher, James Myers, who worked under the name Jimmy DeKnight. Myers, an ambitious man with a single-minded determination to promote himself, has since claimed to have masterminded virtually every successful aspect of Haley's career. Apparently he did have some kind of partnership connection with Howard in Cowboy Records, although he has since claimed ownership of Cowboy without ever mentioning Howard.

'I gave them the name the Saddlemen,' boasts Myers as he sits in his basement office in North Philadelphia. 'I suggested that he go on radio station WPWA. I'm writing a book and it includes much about Bill Haley.'

Myers is also one of the many men connected with Bill Haley who have subsequently claimed to have invented rock & roll. 'I had the first record company in Philadelphia,' says Myers. 'I recorded him because I liked his voice. I recorded them for Center Records, Atlantic Records, Essex Records and so on. Around that time I went into the studio with him and recorded a couple of sides for Atlantic, and I played drums, being a drummer, to give it a lift. I felt it needed more of a lift. So for the first time ever we had drums on a date.' It must be pointed out, however, that Al Rex, the bassist on the session, claims that Myers did not play on the record.

The records in question, 'Why Do I Cry Over You' and 'I'm Gonna Dry Every Tear With A Kiss', were indeed recorded in 1950, the year Haley's first son, Jack, was born. Myers arranged a leasing deal with Atlantic Records, who distributed the disc.

Myers also claims to have given Haley his first steady job, at the Spigot Cafe in Philadelphia. 'Bill comes to me and says I need a steady job, and I said OK. So I booked him into the Spigot Cafe which is the first steady job he ever had. The first night the band opened I was asleep here at home about midnight,

29

the phone rang and it was Billy Ewer and he says 'You've got to get me a new band tomorrow night.' So I had to get up and get dressed and go all the way downtown. I walked in and they were smoking on the stand, drinking on the stand and spending entirely too much time between each number and wearing dirty western clothes.

'So when the set was finished Bill came over and I said "You don't like the job here, do you Bill?" He says "Sure I do, it's our first steady job." I says "Well, then, you're going to have to make some radical changes immediately. No drinking on the stand. You're on forty minutes, off twenty, no smoking on the stand. You wear clean clothes and you type a list of all the songs you know, paste them on the guitar so you can go from one song to the next. Otherwise I'm going to have to let you go tonight." '

Al Rex tells the story differently. 'You know what he did? He got us a job at the Spigot bar and he didn't even have a booking license. He used to split the commission with Jack Howard. Jack Howard had a booking license. We played the Spigot during the Korean War. Our name started getting around because all the sailors would come in at night. So one night John Anthony came in, he owned the Twin Bars in Gloucester. He saw us perform and he hired us. John Anthony heard about us from the sailors.'

Haley's wife Dorothy also recalls Myers. 'The Spigot was a lower class bar,' she says. 'I met Myers a couple of times but I can't remember him having much to do with it, and if he had I surely would have known. I always knew what they were going to do and I can't remember Jim Myers being mentioned, but Lord Jim was around. When Bill came down to visit the kids, Lord Jim would be with him. I think Lord Jim did more for him than anyone. Jack Howard was a good person but he didn't have the contacts he wanted people to think he had. Lord Jim put him on the right track.'

Lord Jim Ferguson was another one of the colorful people hanging around WPWA who would figure in Haley's early career. He ran a morning sports and commentary show on the station and was known around the Chester area, somewhat affectionately as a 'con man's con man'. He liked Haley's band and did what he could to help promote them.

30

According to Dorothy, he did even more than promote them. 'They wanted to make the change from a totally country & western style,' she says, 'but they didn't want to get away from it altogether. So when they came up with this new beat he told them to just change their way of dressing, not to be extreme, and got them into the rock & roll bit. He really got them out of bars, got them down to the seashore and got them going.'

Five: Rock the Joint

'NOW I'D LIKE to pass a message to all of you out there. One . . . two . . . three . . . four . . . What am I counting for? Why, I'm counting to six, just like a new Westinghouse frost free refrigerator. It automatically counts the door openings and when it gets to six begins the defrosting process. Now you can see these amazing new Westinghouse frost free refrigerators . . .'

It was 1951. Bill Haley was sitting in front of the microphone in the tiny WPWA studio, spinning his creamiest announcer spiel. Jack Howard watched him carefully as he talked. Howard was thinking hard.

'. . . So let the Stanley Furniture Company at Fourth and Market streets in Chester show these beautifully, superbly convenient refrigerators,' Haley finished up smoothly. 'They're everything you want in a refrigerator, with giant freeze chests, butter keepers, meat keepers, humidrawer, egg keepers . . .'

Howard was thinking that times were changing. He was thinking about a phone call he'd received from Dave Miller. Miller, a shrewd Philadelphia entrepreneur who owned the Palda record pressing plant, was looking for a local act to cover a song he'd just heard on a trip down south. The song was 'Rocket 88', a hot rhythm & blues tune by Jackie Brenston recorded by another enterprising producer named Sam Phillips. The song was about the late model Oldsmobile, and Miller told Howard he was sure this was the perfect crossover vehicle for the right hillbilly act.

It was time, however, for Haley to plug the upcoming Saddlemen appearance at the Twin Bars. While Haley talked, Howard speculated. Howard knew that Haley's band was doing great with cowboy music but he figured Haley was just about the sharpest young musician he could think of in the area. He told Miller that Haley's band could cover the song but he hadn't broken the news to Bill yet, and he didn't really know how Bill would react to playing blues material.

'So remember friends and neighbors,' Haley continued, 'it doesn't matter where you're from. It doesn't matter whether you're from Delaware, New Jersey, Pennsylvania, if you like hillbilly music and you want continuous western entertainment, the Twin Bars in Gloucester, New Jersey. Drop over and see us will you? Broadway and Market streets in Gloucester. We're looking for a big crowd so come early now will you? Right now friends we have a little bonus tune for you today, Moon Mullican on King Records sings for us "Too Many Irons In the Fire".'

Howard never got around to asking Haley to cover the song that day. But he kept thinking about how the audience reacted when Haley would start the act off, almost as if he were joking, with a blues song called 'Rock the Joint'. The crowd, hillbilly fans, went crazy. Every time.

In February of 1951 'Yodelling Bill Haley' was still playing cowboy matinee shows in Philadelphia. Later in the same year he'd become the first rock & roller – a white man with hillbilly roots playing hard edged blues. 'Rocket 88' was the medium for this fusion, and Dave Miller was the catalyst.

'One day I got a telephone call from a guy named Dave Miller,' Haley later recalled. 'Dave had a little company called Essex Records. He came to me and said "I want to make a record of you, and we'll put it out, but we won't use any pictures, because we don't want people to know if you're black or white." '

In fact Miller hadn't yet formed Essex when 'Rocket 88' was recorded, and the song was originally released on Holiday Records. The Saddlemen first recorded their own arrangement of the song on WPWA, which Miller rejected as having the wrong 'feel', before re-recording it under Miller's direction. The result is certainly unlike anything else Haley ever recorded.

The song opens with sound effects of a car horn blaring followed by the screeching of brakes. Grande's piano leads off with a standard boogie-woogie blues pattern featuring hot right hand figures. Under this introduction Rex slaps a heavy, almost funk pattern on the bass. The rhythmic pace is certainly meatier than any uptempo material the group had previously recorded. The beat is dense and pronounced, a radical departure from their light, airy western swing style recordings. Session guitarist Danny Cedrone accents the pattern with short, staccato chords phrased against the on-beat. When Haley's voice comes in it's with remarkable power – he gives his singing a thick sound against the booming bass line by emphasizing the syllables in grunts and gutteral exclamations rather than singing with his usual clear diction. It's a technique he obviously picked up from r & b vocalists and the surprising thing about it is how well Haley does it, considering he never later returned to even a close approximation of this style.

This is the first significant white interpretation of the postwar r & b form, a fact that could not have been lost on Sam Phillips who, in addition to cutting Brenston's original of the tune at Sun studios in Memphis, employed the same strategy four years later when he launched Elvis Presley to stardom. Amazingly, Haley and the Saddlemen here sound like nothing so much as the early Rolling Stones. The Stones used the same barrelhouse piano framing Mick Jagger's voice formula on some of their first records.

The most striking thing about the song, though, is the powerful relation between Cedrone's guitar and Billy Williamson's brilliant steel playing, a dual guitar concept that marks a stylistic advance which doesn't surface again until Southern rock bands revived the idea twenty years later! Cedrone plays accompaniment until his first solo while Williamson adds gliding fills underneath, then they switch off, Williamson finishing the solo with Cedrone accompanying. After another verse Cedrone takes another full chorus solo, then they repeat the same sequence again, Cedrone finishing with a magnificent run. Haley later told bizarre stories about Miller's methods of stirring the band up to record the kind of rock & roll beat he wanted. Haley told people that Miller took the band to orgies, which they were allowed to watch from a balcony but not to participate in. The idea was to get the band 'worked up' but 'frustrated' enough to play frenzied rock & roll rhythms.

Incredible as this story may seem, it parallels an infamous scandal that surfaced in the Philadelphia area about that time. Haley's description of a kind of small theater where the band

34

was brought to watch orgies corresponds to a place called 'Hound Dog Hill,' where Dick Clark said, in his autobiography, porn films were made.

'There *were* a lot of parties,' recalls James Myers, 'a few I was invited to, but I never went and whether Bill was involved in those or not I don't know. I don't know who was involved because I chose not to go. When I wanted to get laid I picked up the phone or went to a party and there was no problem getting a girl friend. I didn't see the point in going to an orgy and letting everybody knows your business. I know [some guys who] did run some parties and [a] guy who [was associated] with American Bandstand before Dick Clark was involved [with that show].'

Bix Reichner, a Philadelphia area writer whose numerous credits include one of Haley's tunes, 'Mambo Rock', was more explicit. '[One of the guys] was the greatest pussy eater in the world,' he recalls with a laugh. 'He was a real legend. [He] was the first guy who knew how to work payola, the sex and everything. He got in trouble for a lot of things.'

'Rocket 88' was a historic moment in retrospect, but at the time it did little to convince Haley to drop his singing cowboy pose. 'This was an era where there was very strong prejudice in music,' Haley later reminisced. 'If you sang what they called race music, why, you did only that. Or if it was country music, you did only that. A lot of people have said in interviews "You did this deliberately, you were brilliant," but I didn't do it deliberately, I did it out of stupidity. I just didn't realize what I was doing.'

The Saddlemen never returned to the emotional, deliberately unfocused energy of 'Rocket 88', choosing instead to work on a more polished style with 'Greentree Boogie', which again featured an energetic beat but with a simpler lyric and well articulated vocals. At the same time the band continued to turn out traditionally styled country songs like 'Tearstains On My Heart', 'Deep Down In My Heart' and the two-sided Christmas release, 'A Year Ago This Christmas'/'Don't Want To Be Alone This Christmas'. The last record the Saddlemen recorded for Holiday, in early 1952, was called 'Jukebox Cannonball', a remake of the country standard with jived-up lyrics that showed Haley returning to his hillbilly crossover tactics. In early '52 Haley cut his first single for Miller's newly formed Essex label.

35

The song was 'Icy Heart', an idea meant to capitalize on the success of Hank Williams' '51 tearjerker, 'Cold, Cold Heart'. Haley had reached his peak as a vocalist – he could handle just about any style at this point, although he seemed most at home with country ballads – and the Saddlemen felt that 'Icy Heart' might well be the breakthrough they'd been looking for.

Jack Howard still couldn't forget the audience reaction to Haley's version of 'Rock the Joint' at the Twin Bar, and he suggested that the Saddlemen should cover the song as the B-side of 'Icy Heart'. Miller agreed and this time he let Haley and the Saddlemen use their own arrangement and performance style. The sound has a similar energy to the driving beat of 'Rocket 88' but it's much cleaner, and Haley articulates each word in his delivery clearly, clipping each line off against the rhythm pattern.

Miller employed one interesting new device in the recording of 'Rock the Joint' which marked a turning point in the development of rock & roll. 'Rock the Joint' featured the first use of the 'slapback bass' sound that is central to the non-drum percussive style of early rockabilly. In fact Al Rex had been employing this percussive technique, in which the sound of the player's hand hitting the neck of the bass and the rattling of the strings drove the rhythm, for a while. You can hear a less pronounced version of the style on 'Yodel Your Blues Away', and on 'Rocket 88', for example. Miller's contribution was to record it in such a way that it became one of the predominate sounds in the mix.

'I was the instigator of rock & roll,' says Al Rex. 'When we were down at WPWA I had this old bass fiddle that did not have a sound post. When I used to slap it you didn't hear no tone, all you used to hear was clickety-click-click-click. So when we were recording down at the radio station I asked Dave Miller "How do you want me to do it?" and I started slapping the bass; clickety-clickety-clickety-click. Dave Miller said "That's what I want to hear!" He said "Put the microphone on that bass. Let's get that sound." That was the start of it.'

Haley himself looked back on his recording of 'Rock the Joint' as the beginning of rock & roll. 'This is the true story about how the original rock thing came about,' he said. 'I was working over in a nightclub in New Jersey called the Twin Bars. It was near the Philadelphia Navy Yard, and a lot of the young

Navy guys used to come there. It was their hangout. It always seemed like we really rocked the place, unknowingly – we were supposed to be a country band. I did a live country show on WPWA, and just before my show there was a show called 'Judge Rhythm's Court,' which was a two-hour disc jockey show by a guy named Jim Reeves.

'Jim was white, but he played all race music. I used to listen to this show while I was getting ready and that probably influenced me a lot too. He used a tune called "Rock the Joint" as a theme. It was strictly a race record. I started to sing and hum the tune, and I started to use it in the show, and every time I would do it I would see this tremendous reaction. So I rewrote some of the lyrics, released the record and it became a big smash hit for us.'

Haley recalled that he made it as a rock & roller just as his ambition to become a major country artist was close to realization. 'The initial recording that was a hit was "Icy Heart". I began receiving many offers as a country and western artist. I went out on the road promoting "Icy Heart" and got to Nashville with hopes of going on the Grand Old Opry, and I got a phone call from Dave Miller in the hotel room that evening telling me to get off the "Icy Heart" side and get on "Rock the Joint", because that was hitting.

'I did, and we were faced with a great problem, because I had never in years thought that this would happen. What was I going to do? Here I was with the sideburns, cowboy boots and almost ten years of promoting myself as a country and western singer. You have to remember that the public in general wasn't ready to accept this – the prejudice was tremendous.'

Haley's first attempts to play rock & roll to audiences that had come specifically to hear that kind of music were disasters. 'I had to go out, and at first there was great disappointment among blacks that I wasn't black, and great disappointment for the whites – plus a complete new style of music.'

One can imagine how a rhythm & blues audience might have reacted to a band of rural Pennsylvania cowboys that played a hybrid cowboy blues. 'The first big booking we got,' Haley recalled, 'was in Chicago at a jazz club. Dizzy Gillespie had just finished, and we went in and I had the number one record in the city. But people would come in for one song and just get up and

37

leave. After three nights I cancelled out because it was a tough thing for a kid to take.'

Bill Haley was getting his first taste of the price of fame. It was a cruel irony for him to have been on the brink of realizing his childhood dream of becoming a successful singing cowboy only to be thrown off by a major breakthrough in an unfamiliar field. It's easy to understand why he went along with the idea of releasing records without identifying pictures – he didn't consider himself particularly handsome and was obviously self-conscious about his blind eye. But when the result of that strategy was that he was rejected and ridiculed by hostile audiences, Haley was faced with a bitter dilemma.

Haley had little time to consider this double bind before a wholly unexpected element entered the picture. Black audiences may not have accepted his color, white audiences may not have accepted his music, but there was another audience that would come into play – kids. 'Previous to "Rock the Joint" we used to get mail from all the hillbillies from Bridgetown and Vineland, New Jersey, places like that,' Al Rex points out. 'Now all of a sudden this record comes out and all the disc jockeys flipped it over. They start playing "Rock the Joint". Next thing you know we start getting mail from all the high school kids up in Norristown and Phoenixville. Now this was the start of it.'

For Rex, it was also the end of it. He dropped out of touring and recording with the Saddlemen to put together his own group, although he continued to play with the Saddlemen on their noon-to-one radio show, and when Haley later quit the show he turned it over to Rex. 'We were playing around but we weren't making any money,' Rex recalls, 'so I formed my own trio. This was when they took Lord Jim in as a partner in place of me.'

That wasn't the only shakeup in Haley's life at the time. The pressures of his hectic social existence placed an intolerable strain on his marriage. He and Dorothy filed for divorce. 'Our divorce was by mutual agreement,' Dorothy later said. 'No bad feelings, it was just that, hey, why hang on this way? It wasn't doing either one of us any good.'

Haley immediately remarried. His second wife, Barbara Joan Cupchack, was a pretty, young, Monroe-style blonde. 'Cuppy,' as she was nicknamed, knew Haley's first wife because the two had seen each other at Haley's live performances. 'It's hard for me to paint her good when I can't, really,' Dorothy hesitated in recalling her experiences with Cuppy. 'If it hadn't been her it would have been another young girl. He had young girls chasing him constantly, they just fell right at him and he was there. This is what broke up our marriage really. He was very susceptible to them.'

Haley's second wife presented him with a baby girl, Joanie, later in the year.

KEYSTONE RECORDS

ASCAP MYERS MUSIC
I'M NOT TO BLAME
(Bill Borrelli, Jr.)
BILL HALEY
and THE SADDLE MEN
with
Billy Williamson
(STEEL GUITAR)
5102-B

HOLIDAY RECORDS

N.M.P.C.
BMI
Time—2:30
Mfgd. by
PALDA RECORD CO.
Phila., Penna.

ROCKET "88"
(Brenston)
BILL HALEY
and
THE SADDLEMEN
105-A

HOLIDAY RECORDS
DISC-JOCKEY COPY

HALEY-HOWARD PUB.
BMI
(H-108A)
Mfgd. by
PALDA RECORD CO.
PHILA., PENNA.

GREEN TREE BOOGIE
(Haley)
BILL HALEY
and the
SADDLEMEN
108

HOLIDAY RECORDS

Jem Publications
ASCAP
Mfgd. by
PALDA RECORD CO.
Phila., Penna.

**I DON'T WANT TO BE
ALONE FOR CHRISTMAS**
Menaker - D'Onofrio - Russell
BILL HALEY
and
THE SADDLEMEN
111

HOLIDAY RECORDS

Jack Howard, Pub.
BMI
Time - 2:13
(H-113A)
Manufactured by
PALDA RECORD CO.
Phila., Pa.

JUKE BOX CANNON BALL
(Rogers - Keefer - Barrie)
BILL HALEY
with
THE SADDLEMEN
113-A

HOLIDAY RECORDS

Halley - Howard, Pub.
BMI
(H-110B)
Manufactured by
PALDA RECORD CO.
Phila., Pa.

SUNDOWN BOOGIE
(Haley - Rogers)
BILL HALEY
with
THE SADDLEMEN
113-B

ESSEX RECORDS

Success Music
BMI
(E-303A)

ICY HEART
(Berk - Berk)
BILL HALEY
with
The Saddlemen
303

MFGD. IN U.S.A. BY PALDA RECORD CO., 8406 LYONS AVE., PHILA., PENNA.

ESSEX RECORDS

Andrea Music
BMI
(E-303B)

ROCK THE JOINT
(Crafton - Keene - Bagby)
BILL HALEY
with
The Saddlemen
303

MFGD. IN U.S.A. BY PALDA RECORD CO., 8406 LYONS AVE., PHILA., PENNA.

Labels of early 78 rpm Keystone, Holiday, Essex records
by Bill Haley and the Saddlemen

Six: Change Is Now

WITHOUT QUESTION, 'ROCK the Joint' marked the beginning of the age of rock & roll. The song was the first national hit to become an anthem for schoolkids who refused to make the limited choice of listening to segregated music. It was a song about having such a good time that nothing mattered: 'We're gonna tear down the mailbox, rip up the floor/Smash out the windows and knock down the door.' It featured the first great rock & roll guitar solo, a fiery lead played by Danny Cedrone as the third chorus that was so good it was later reproduced virtually note-for-note as the solo on 'Rock Around the Clock.'

It was time to hang up the spurs.

They made one more record under the name of the Saddlemen, 'Rocking Chair on the Moon' with 'Dance with a Dolly' on the B-side. 'Rocking Chair on the Moon' was slower paced than 'Rock the Joint' and featured a Hawaiian guitar sound. Haley's perfunctory vocal is nothing special, but Billy Williamson's beautiful steel guitar accompaniment is the main voice. This was the song in which Williamson first used the 'telegraph style' steel playing, where he phrased short staccato bursts against the rhythm. His tremendous steel solo on this track switches from fluid runs to that percussive technique. 'Williamson was only a hillbilly steel guitar player,' Al Rex points out. 'But when he started playing rock & roll he did it really different, his playing became very inventive.'

'Dance with a Dolly' was a novelty tune based on the popular song 'Buffalo Gal'. It was an obvious combination of the cornpone roots of Haley's singing cowboy persona with his growing realization that there was some kind of formula to pop success. Exactly what this formula was eluded Haley—all he knew was that he had tapped it with 'Rock the Joint'. Over the

40

next few years Haley would run through a variety of ideas in his attempt to figure out what this formula for success might be. Several elements of 'Dance with a Dolly' became recurrent themes in later songs. One was Haley's repeated use of hipster jive buzz words as lyric keys – in this case, 'I'm Gone' and the line 'Gonna rock and stomp 'till the break of dawn'. This was also his first of many adaptions of nursery rhymes and pop tunes to a rock & roll beat, a strategy based on the idea that vague familiarity is the key to commercial appeal.

'We came back to Philadelphia,' Haley later explained, 'and I started to write tunes on this idea and the word "rock" kept coming up. I wrote a tune for a group called the Esquire Boys and there was a group called the Treniers. They were friends of mine, and asked me to write something for them, so I wrote a song called "Rock-a-Beatin-Boogie", and there's a line in the song that goes "Rock, rock, rock, everybody/roll, roll roll everybody". It was recorded by the Esquire Boys and also by the Treniers for Columbia Records. I didn't record it myself at that time.'

Meanwhile Jim Ferguson, who'd taken over completely from Jack Howard as Haley's manager and replaced Al Rex as the fourth partner in the organization, was promoting up a storm. 'Lord Jim went around to all these schools in the area,' Rex recalls. 'They were doing assemblies for free so Lord Jim used to set this up.' Ferguson booked the group into the kind of places they'd never played before. 'Jim knew a guy down in Stone Harbor, New Jersey, and he sold Haley to this alcoholic guy who owned the Stone Harbor cafe for the summer. This was the first time they had a hillbilly band down there. They played down there all summer. Next thing you know John Anthony at the Twin Bars wants them back. Well all of a sudden the price went up.' The Stone Harbor residence was the beginning of Haley's association with the Atlantic seacoast summer resorts centered around Wildwood and Atlantic City, New Jersey.

A new image was in order. Ferguson had also been trying to work the band into the Philadelphia lounges so the decision to adopt matching tuxedos to replace the cowboy gear made sense. 'They were trying to break into another circuit,' said Rex, 'the Philadelphia band circuit. They wanted to break out of the hillbilly circuit. How the hell can Bill Haley go to lounges

41

dressed in a cowboy hat? So he finally got into the tuxedos. Even later, though, he was still a hillbilly at heart. We had to tell him not to wear white socks with the tuxedo.'

All the band needed to complete the new look was a snazzy name. Bix Reichner, another of the WPWA disc jockeys who hosted a big band show on the station, was also a songwriter. He knew Haley and Ferguson were looking for new material, and having heard Haley's 'Dance with a Dolly' he also knew what they wanted. He took them a song called 'Stop Beating around the Mulberry Bush,' which Haley snapped up for his next record. 'Y'know,' said Reichner, half-joking, 'with a name like Haley, you ought to call your group the Comets.'

Bill Haley and the Comets recorded their first song, 'Stop Beating around the Mulberry Bush', which was virtually identical to the last tune they did as the Saddlemen, 'Dance with a Dolly'. The only difference was that for the first time they used a drummer, Dick Richards, on the session. Richards played a brief drum roll for the intro, an occasional rim shot and a march solo for eight bars just before the final flourish, but aside from those details the rhythm of the song was still carried by the bass. The song also contains Haley's first self-referential lyric: 'Better begin to rock the joint'. Later on he would often use the device of repeating titles from previous hits in the lyrics to songs.

Haley's next record, 'Crazy Man, Crazy,' was the breakthrough. It was one of the hottest songs of the summer of 1953, putting Haley, and rock & roll, on the map for the first time in a big way. The calculation of its construction reveals the process Haley was trying out to formularize rock & roll.

In fact, 'Crazy Man, Crazy' is little more than a catalogue of effects. This time there's a longer, more elaborate and dramatic drum solo intro as well as more drumming inside the main arrangement of the song, although it's still the bass pushing the beat. The novelty concept is introduced in Cedrone's guitar solo, which flirts with the melodic line of 'Dixie'. Once again the lyrics rely heavily on jive phrases and buzz words like 'crazy, man, crazy' and 'man, that music's gone'.

For the first time in 'Crazy Man, Crazy' Haley projects the sense of knowing the audience he's aiming for. He's definitely outside of and dictating to a specific audience when he points out in one line: 'To keep *them* rocking all you've got to say is ...' This calculation is carried through masterfully by the shouted backing chorus, which adopts the stance of the fans while at the same time cueing them, yelling 'Go, go, go everybody' before exploding into a wild, anarchic scream. The device cleverly invites audience participation on the most basic level, and to judge from the frantic fan reaction, especially around the Philadelphia-to-Baltimore area, it worked brilliantly. So even though the song ends awkwardly and in general lacks the clarity and punch of 'Rock the Joint', it puts all the elements together to coin a rock & roll concept with mass appeal.

However, it would be a mistake to attribute 'Crazy Man, Crazy's' success solely to the brilliance of its conception. Dave Miller's relentless promotional ability was instrumental in making the song such a big hit. 'Miller was a genius as a promoter and a shrewd business man,' says Bix Reichner. 'He made millions and blew a lot of it back. There was no doubt that Miller would take over because he was a real operator.'

'I'll tell you this much,' says Al Rex, 'he was a money maker. He was out for money. When we first started out Miller took Haley around to a few cities and he bought savings bonds for the jocks and paid them off to play the record, whatever record we had out. What Miller used to do was he had his pressing plant and when the stores would call up and want to buy so much of one record he'd say "Well, you have to buy so much of Haley too".'

Haley recalled 1953 as the beginning of his stardom. 'As we got into the rock & roll field,' he told Ken Terry, 'we got rid of the boots, the sideburns and the cowboy hats. We wore tuxedos and we became the Comets. I got my first Cadillac, and everything I touched seemed to turn to gold. I was riding high on "Crazy Man, Crazy".

'This is the period that there's been a lot of controversy about. But this is actually what happened. There was a guy in Cleveland named Alan Freed, working on a local station up there. Alan had a show called the "Moon Dog Show". I had never met him. I had a good friend named Bill Randall in Cleveland at that time and Alan was just starting his career. As his opening song he would use "Rock-a-Beatin'-Boogie," which started out "Rock, rock, rock everybody/Roll, roll, roll every-

43

body" and Alan would pound on the desk and shout "Rock!! Rock!! Rock & roll everybody!!" with the record.

'This was a couple of years when everything was exploding. This was when Elvis was still in Memphis listening to Bill Haley records on the jukebox. There was a time when I had one hit after another, they were releasing them every eight or ten weeks. We were just swamped with offers, we were playing everywhere we could – in high schools and wherever you play.'

Haley's memory glossed over the fact that the year following 'Crazy Man, Crazy' was marked by infighting between his handlers and an inability to come up with a suitable follow-up hit. If 'Crazy Man, Crazy' demonstrated Haley's ability to coin a successful formula, the next song, 'Pat-a-Cake', proved how little Haley had really grasped of what made it work. Here the most trite nursery rhyme imaginable was turned into a very unsuitable rock & roll medium. Bicycle bell and winding clock sound effects frame the tune, Haley shouts 'I'm gone' unconvincingly, the drummer adds a few cowbell accents and Cedrone references 'Dixie' again in such a poor solo that you know he was not thrilled with the idea. The tune was insincere and forced, one of the few truly bad performances by the band, which usually played well even on the worst material. The flip side, 'Fractured', was much better, but not enough to offset the damage of 'Pat-a-Cake'. The rest of the year they released a series of unsuccessful songs: 'Live It Up', 'Farewell So Long Goodbye', 'I'll Be True to You', 'Ten Little Indians', 'Straight Jacket' and 'Chatanooga Choo-Choo'. This motley collection of bad ideas and corny, comically stilted performances (the vocal chorus on 'I'll Be True to You' sounds like a drunken sing-along at a men's smoker) did little to enhance Haley's reputation.

Meanwhile, the obvious next step after 'Crazy Man, Crazy' was staring everyone in the face. Veteran songwriter Max Freedman had written a song in partnership with Jim Myers, 'Rock Around the Clock', that was better suited to Haley than anything since 'Rock the Joint'. It had been a proven crowd pleaser at places like the Broomall Cafe, where Haley's six month residence brought out a frenzied audience of student fans night after night, and along the heavy partying summer shores of Wildwood, New Jersey, where Haley was anticipating the surf music movement by a full ten years.

Ralph Jones, who later became the Comets' drummer, remembers Haley's version of 'Rock Around the Clock' being big at Wildwood in the summer of '53, and points out that a lot of people liked it because it resembled a number of r&b tunes about all-night sex.

Miller refused to let Haley record the song, and his reason seemed to be a clash with Jim Myers, who was promoting 'Rock Around the Clock' as Haley's next big hit. 'Jimmy and Dave Miller didn't like each other,' Haley said. 'Three times I took the tune into the recording studio and put it on the music rack, and every time Miller would see it, he'd come in and tear it up and throw it away. So I never could record it. I wanted to – had it rehearsed and all – but he just absolutely refused because of his dislike for Myers.'

Myers recalls pretty much the same story. 'I wrote "Rock Around the Clock" with the late Max Freedman and I had Haley in mind at the time so when I gave it to him he flipped over. He knew instantly it was for him. But when he took it in to the company he was working for at the time the guy tore it up and said it will never sell. He didn't have any belief in it.'

In the end, though, it was Myers who won, because when Haley's contract with Essex ran out the group decided to get a deal with a new label. Miller had seemed to lose interest anyway. He was making a lot of money with his new idea, the 101 Strings.

Seven: The Sun Never Shines In Studio A

WHEN HALEY AND the Comets left Essex, Jim Myers stepped in to oversee the group's transition to a new label. His mind was on the hit potential of 'Rock Around the Clock,' and beyond that, the lucrative publishing deal that he might be able to make. He arrived at the shrewd and absolutely crucial decision to go to Milt Gabler, head of artist acquisitions and chief producer for Decca Records. Decca was at the time one of the three giant record companies in the industry along with Columbia and RCA.

At that point Gabler was the only man at a major label who understood rock & roll. He had been in the vanguard of creative musical developments ever since he started the nation's first independent label, Commodore, to record jazz artists. Gabler recorded Billie Holiday, Eddie Condon, Peewee Russell, Meade Lux Lewis and a host of others until Jack Kapp, the president of Decca Records, hired him in 1941.

At Decca Gabler recorded greats like Louis Armstrong, Ella Fitzgerald and the Ink Spots. Some of Gabler's greatest recordings, though, were of Louis Jordan, the popular postwar bandleader whose hot dance music yielded such important pre-rock rhythm & blues hits as 'Caldonia' and 'Choo Choo Ch-Boogie'. Many early rock & roll figures, Chuck Berry in particular, credit Jordan with inspiring the rhythm and arrangement sense for much of rock & roll. Jordan's career had tailed off in the early '50s and finally he left Decca in 1953. Gabler certainly had an idea that rock & roll was waiting in the wings, and when Myers brought Haley's availability to his attention Gabler knew he'd found what he was looking for.

'I was aware that rock was starting,' Gabler recalls. 'I knew what was happening in the Philadelphia area, and "Crazy Man,

Crazy" had been a hit about a year before that. It already was starting and I wanted to take it from there.

'Jim Myers made the appointment to see me and brought Bill in from Philadelphia. Miller thought that no one else in the world could record Bill Haley the way he recorded him on Essex and Jim Myers promptly brought Haley to me because either somebody had told him or he felt that Milt Gabler could make. the records as well. So he brought a few releases on Essex and played them for me. I said "If I couldn't make a record as good as that or even better I wouldn't be sitting in this chair".'

Gabler signed Haley on the spot. On 12th April 1954, Haley arrived with his band at Decca's Pythian Temple studio in New York to make a historic recording. The band consisted of Haley, Cedrone, Williamson, Grande, Marshall Lytle and a session drummer that Gabler insisted on using, Billy Guesack. They recorded two songs – 'Thirteen Women,' an r & b tune by Dickie Thompson, and '(We're Gonna) Rock Around the Clock'.

The sound was cleaner, more consistent, more professional and brighter than anything Miller had cut. The arrangements were also far more sophisticated than the Essex material. The corniness and crude, kitchen-sink approach to including catchy gimmicks was replaced by slick, big-band style arrangements where every part played a crucial role. 'Thirteen Women', a wierd novelty tune about the aftermath of an atomic holocaust that leaves one man and thirteen women alive, was very close to the Louis Jordan style. A riffing saxophone and brushed drums carried the rhythm with the guitar slicing in great little jazz fills and Haley singing what was for him a pretty emotional vocal. The slap-back bass wasn't introduced until the break for the guitar solo, the steel guitar was anonymous, used only for unison playing when its sound would be masked, and Grande's piano got only one cameo passage. This kind of musical editing was previously missing from Haley's arrangements, and had to be Gabler's influence on the group.

'(We're Gonna) Rock Around the Clock' was an inspired performance on that day and remains as vital nearly thirty years later. It's no accident that this song provided the pivot point for rock & roll's recognition and mass acceptance. Guesak's three snare drum rim shots usher in the era of rock & roll. Haley chants the invocation:

47

One-two-*three* o'clock, four o'clock *rock*
(Guesak hits another rim shot. Haley sings the next line a tone higher.)
    Five-six-*seven* o'clock, eight o'clock *rock*
(Another shot: Haley accelerates the tensions by straining up to the next note.)
    Nine-ten-*leven* o'clock, twelve o'clock *rock*
    We're gonna *rock* a-*round* the *clock* to-*night!*

The band bursts into a full out, boogie dance pattern with guitars, saxophone and piano hitting blaring, single note riffs against the popping bass rhythm, with Guesack smacking a double rim shot on the backbeat at the end of each line. Cedrone proceeds to duplicate his great solo from 'Rock the Joint'. This is the solo that inspired a generation of rock guitarists. 'Phew, that's the solo that made that guitar famous, the Black Beauty fretless wonder,' says rockabilly revivalist Rob Stoner. 'If you can play that last part, the four bars when it goes from the five chord to the four chord, you can pick pretty fast.'

The song is structured so that each successive verse turns the screw tighter, building to a manic frenzy that bursts wide open when the saxophone leads a unison riffing chorus with guitars and piano flailing against a sustained drum roll. It's a moment of pure genius that encapsulates the music's fire and drama for all time. 'Rock Around the Clock' has subsequently become the national anthem of rock & roll, the largest selling rock & roll hit in history, having run through some thirty million copies by more than 100 different groups.

No version of this song has ever topped the original. For that moment in time Haley's band had a spirit, a sense of summing up what had gone before and arriving at a new level, that can never be duplicated. You can reproduce the song, as Haley later did, note for note and still be missing something.

Perhaps not surprisingly, James E. Myers takes the credit for 'Rock Around the Clock's' magic sound. 'I sat on a chair leaning against the wall smoking one of my cigars, and Milt Gabler sat next to me leaning against the wall smoking one of my cigars, and there were two gray-haired engineers, that looked like they worked for Edison they were so old, working the knobs.

'When I suggested certain things that could be done to

improve the arrangements they went along with them and then when I got back in the control booth I got so excited that I yelled at the two engineers "Peak! Peak!" Both of them swivelled their heads looking at me in horror, because they had never heard that word before to be done deliberately. They were professional engineers. Milt just moved his cigar up and down to do what I wanted because he didn't care, I was on the B side for all intents and purposes as far as he was concerned. "Rock Around the Clock" was not going to be the hit, he had the hit on the other side. So he just moved his cigar up and down to do what I told them so they let the needle ride into the red for the first time ever by any engineers on Decca Records. You bet your bottom dollar.

'They just shrugged their shoulders and did what they were told and deliberately distorted the record because that's the way I heard it. And the rest is history. Now they do it deliberately all the time.'

Milt Gabler, as you might imagine, recalls the occasion differently. 'He didn't produce the recordings. Being an active participant in the signing of Bill, of course he was present on the day we recorded. And he could have come into the control room to hear playbacks. But he didn't produce the record. I would never allow anyone to take charge of a record date. It was my job. I was responsible for the recording, the sound of it and everything and if anyone would interfere I would stop him. Or ask him to leave the control room.

'It's possible he might have said, the same as anyone else that's interested, make it louder or do something. But he had no control over the engineer. He couldn't give orders to anyone to do anything. Simultaneously I could be thinking the same thing that he was when he's standing next to me. But the engineer wouldn't move it at his command or do anything for anyone except me.

'Everybody wants the credit, including me. But I made the records.'

However, Myers did allow in his recollections for Gabler's authority. 'Milt was in charge, no question about it, and the engineers did their job and knew it, did it well. But I would make suggestions here and there and they were always adopted.'

Gabler has another idea about 'Rock Around the Clock's'

success. 'There are what I call natural songs. There are certain songs that when you record them, you know they're gonna be hit songs so you'd better as an A&R man make the best possible damn record you can make of that song. Otherwise Victor will make a better one, or Capitol, whatever label. So you put your best ingredients together and you take them into the studio and add what you can add yourself, and you hope it comes out the best record on the song, all you can do is try. During the year you might find three or four of those natural hits. The rest are created, but some songs are so good you can't even destroy them.'

Gabler pointed out that 'Rock Around the Clock' is an old blues. 'My Daddy Rocks Me with a Steady Roll' that's where rock & roll came from, from the lyrics of that song. It's just a re-write of it with a change of tune. I always loved that tune. It's a natural hit, that kind of a song. Haley created the white rock & roll, teenage rock & roll. It might have been derived from black music or country and western music but it didn't have that beat that Bill imparted to it. I think he really created it, when he played down in Wildwood, New Jersey.'

'Rock Around the Clock' sold 75,000 copies right off the bat in 1954. Decca was delighted. 'We re-signed the band,' recalls Gabler. 'Picked up their option right away.' If Gabler had any doubts about Haley's potential, 'Rock Around the Clock' dispelled them.

They needed a follow-up, and Gabler arranged for another session on 7th June. Haley had never made two good recordings in a row, and 'Rock Around the Clock' had been sitting around for a while, so the challenge of coming up with hot new material was great. Myers had made a verbal agreement with Haley to record one of the songs he published during each session. That was fine as long as the material was of the caliber of 'Rock Around the Clock', but for the second session Myers pawned off an unmitigated piece of hackwork called 'ABC Boogie' on Haley. The song was lame, phony and trite. What's more, it offered the kids who'd found an identity in the raucous fun of 'Rock the Joint', 'Crazy Man, Crazy' and 'Rock Around the Clock' a jive moralization about being taught by a teacher with a boogie beat.

Fortunately Haley had the sense to pick a really hot song for the A-side of the second session, Charles E. Calhoun's tremendous 'Shake, Rattle and Roll,' which was a sizeable r&b hit by Joe Turner. This was even closer to the kind of songs Gabler had produced for Louis Jordan and proved the perfect vehicle to match Haley's ideas and abilities with Gabler's expertise.

Gabler's production of the tune took the Ahmet Ertegun/ Jerry Wexler version head on. The Turner cut was stark, with simple instrumental backing to accent the singer's dynamic voice. Comparison between the two versions virtually defines rock & roll – Turner's is a blues, Haley's is pure rock & roll.

The tempo of Gabler's production, for a start, is crisper. The slap-back bass is so energetic it makes the walking bass line of the Ertegun/Wexler production sound dull by comparison. The honking sax riff that kicks off the tune and answers each line of the verse is a dramatic improvement over the subdued horn arrangement on the Atlantic release. Unlike other Haley tunes there is no guitar solo. Instead guitars, sax and keyboards slam away on a unison chorus with the whole band repeatedly shouting 'Go!' for an effect that caught lightning in a bottle. In fact the band's backing vocals, which so often sound forced and uninspired, are truly exciting here and seem to spur Haley on to what is probably the vocal performance of his life. The distance from the material he usually exhibits is replaced here by an urgency that has him actually straining to push his high notes on the chorus.

Prevailing critical sentiment holds that Turner's version is superior to Haley's, but while allowing for the obvious fact that Turner was unquestionably the better vocalist, the Gabler production is far more exciting than Atlantic's release. There certainly were many cases where white artists covered black r&b hits with inferior versions that were successful simply because the singer was the right color. But to dismiss all white cover versions is also racism—the Bill Haley cover of 'Shake Rattle and Roll' sold more copies than Turner's because it was a better record.

Gabler went so far as to insist that Haley wasn't a cover artist on this record. 'I call it the switch treatment,' he said. 'In other words if you can't chase the original record you do a switch. To go for a different market, you do it by Louis Jordan or you do it by the Ink Spots rather than – we used to cover Frank Sinatra hits with the Ink Spots, to get the juke boxes in the black markets in the days when the Ink Spots sold. Of course you never could catch Sinatra so you go for part of the market.'

At the point when he made 'Shake Rattle and Roll' Gabler didn't realize how big the rock & roll part of the market would become. The song took the country, and most of the world, by storm. It was the first rock record to sell a million copies, and it firmly established Haley as a teen hero despite the fact that he was pushing thirty. But it wasn't just kids that responded to the pulsing, thumping crash of the song. A professional ice hockey team, the Springfield Indians of the American Hockey League, adopted 'Shake Rattle and Roll' as their fight song and played it on the arena loudspeaker before and after every home game and after every goal they scored.

Another key to the success of Haley's version of 'Shake Rattle and Roll' was the clean-up job Gabler performed on the lyrics. The original was frankly sexual, and Gabler made several adjustments. Where Turner sings 'The way you wear those dresses, the sun comes shining through,' Haley sings 'Wearin' those dresses, your hair done up so nice'. Where Turner boasts 'I can look at you till you ain't no child no more,' Haley complains 'I can look at you and tell you don't love me no more'.

'If any of the lyrics were double entendre I would clean them up,' Gabler explains. 'I didn't want any censor with the radio station to bar the record from being played on the air. With NBC a lot of the race records wouldn't get played on the air because of the lyrics. So I had to watch that closely.' Having produced the Ink Spots and Louis Jordan, Gabler knew what would pass the censors.

When Haley and the Comets came to Decca, Gabler had a specific approach to recording them already worked out. 'I had expected a band like that,' he explains. 'They weren't schooled musicians. They were good players. They learned it by rote. They were tremendous. They didn't play written arrangements. If they goofed in the middle of a song you couldn't say let's take it from the ninth bar or the seventeenth bar or two beats before that. You had to go back to the intro and start from the top and go all over again until you finally got a complete take all the way through that didn't have imperfections in it and had the spirit you wanted. It would take us about half a day to do one tune.

Today that's nothing with rock groups. I would book a studio for the entire day and by five or six o'clock I got in three tunes and that was terrific. I would always try to at least get two so we'd have a record to release.'

Gabler's memories of Haley's sessions with him are marvellously detailed and analytical. He got the band to sound as good as they did by rehearsing them meticulously. 'They got it down,' he says. 'Johnny Grande was supposed to keep the thing together. If they were looking for a chord for the steel guitar Johnny would have to hit it on the piano and they'd have to pick up their notes by ear. I'd sing the riffs. It wasn't just Jordan's riffs. It was everyday business to me. You hum a riff to the guys. The jazz fellows used to do it, not just Jordan.

'Being a producer of jazz records and Louis Jordan I used all the riffs that the little swing bands played that Jordan knew and were heard on 52nd street where I grew up. I used the jazz riffs that the sax players and the trombone sections and all of them come up with as background. I used to create the Haley arrangements. I used to hum the licks to them and they'd work out the parts. Things like barber shop quartet singers. They'd work out their own harmony. But when they learned a riff they'd learn it by rote and boy when they had that down it used to rock.

'All of the backgrounds had to have figures and it had to be a figure that a guy could take a solo against. It was mostly for harmonies, we would hum the riffs and try to use the piano to explain it to them. They'd play it and try and put the notes together. I'd say, no, that doesn't sound good, look for other notes, because I'm an ear musician also. I'd say I don't like the sound, voice it differently. Then they'd go to the piano and fool around. They'd get it, then we'd get the old lick going and, boy, when they got it down it was good. Then up to the next eight or twelve bars we'd change it to something so it kept building. Then I would have Billy Williamson hit what I'd call lightning flashes on the steel guitar. He'd put the bar across it and go Pow! Pow! It was like brass.'

One of the big reasons Gabler's rock & roll productions sounded so good was the unusual studio used for the recordings, the Pythian Temple in New York. The huge, completely round room with high, vaulted ceilings provided a naturally dynamic sound for rock records. 'It was a converted ballroom,' Gabler explains. 'It was in a building that used to belong to the Knights of Pithius which is a fraternal organization. They had fallen on bad times and they used to lease it. We leased the ballroom. It had a balcony in it, a very high ceiling, a beautiful wood floor. We used it for the natural reverb, the natural sound you got in there. We converted it into a recording studio, built a control room in one corner, put in a stage.

'We'd have invited audiences. A few writers might come up the time of a Haley session. Actually they were closed sessions. Sammy Davis would always have a big audience but with Bill Haley there would be almost no one there.

'We recorded on one track, mono recordings. We used the natural sound of the room plus we took the kitchen and made over the kitchen adjacent where they used to cater any affairs in the ballroom. It was nothing but a bunch of old tables and chairs and it was like a storage room. We made that into an echo chamber. So we used the natural sound of the room plus taped echo, tape reverb. We'd put one microphone on Bill, one on drums, one on the piano . . . one for each instrument. We didn't use flats or anything. There was no separation between the instruments, we just placed the fellows on the stage. Bill didn't have a very strong voice. His voice never had a cutting edge to it, that cuts through the band. He had to sing very close to the mike and therefore I didn't put him up with the band. I put him on the floor in front of the band which would have been three and a half or four feet below them really because they were up on stage. It was like a little theater without seats, and he would be in the orchestra down on the dance floor in front of the band. They all had their own mikes, although I think the steel guitar and tenor were picked up on the same mike.'

The drum rim-shot became an important element on these sessions. 'You got that echo from the room's high ceiling when the stick would hit the rim of the drum on a rimshot. It wasn't a phony echo, just a natural sound. Haley would be eight feet in front of the rest of the band down below and it would probably pick up just right on his vocal mike. It all worked together.

'If the background singing was weak we'd get them all around the mike, play the tape back and cut another tape with them all singing the group parts. But Bill voice always went on first, at the same time we did the rhythm. I always thought you get a much better feeling that way. I hated years later when the accompaniment track was made first and then a good singer would come in with earphones and sing with a track. When I had a band behind singers they sang, you know, they could feel the arrangement. When you have it pinched down in your earphones I don't see how you can get excitement from the accompaniment.'

Haley's guitar playing was not an important part of the arrangement. 'It didn't bother me,' says Gabler. 'He kept time right. He wasn't a fancy guitarist, but he could play the chords of the songs. That's simple chords anyway, but he might have even stopped playing at certain parts. I don't know, because we had the rhythm going so strong. But I always liked the rhythm guitar in with the rhythm section, to blend in with the afterbeat of the drums. All he did was play afterbeat guitar. But he would need it to keep himself in tune. All singers that play guitar, it's just to keep themselves in tune. But he wouldn't use his guitar the way some great guitarists do to show the guys what he wants. He just used it to accompany his singing. But when they got it down it rocked, I'll tell you that.'

Eight: The Golden Age of Rock & Roll

BILL HALEY WAS the king of rock & roll by the summer of 1954. 'You know how people jump on the bandwagon,' he would later recall. 'This just exploded tremendously in show business in general, because here was a kid from nowhere who had something that revolutionized the business because it was basically easy to do. Everyone could do it, every record company and a million artists, among them Elvis Presley, Pat Boone and all of them. And this is the reason of course that the music became so big.

'I hit the music business,' Haley reasoned, 'when everything was confused. The big band era had faded, the day of the solo vocalist – Perry Como and so forth – had gone by. The only thing happening at the time was progressive jazz. That's fine music, but the public wasn't buying it, and the people were ready for something. I came in with something simple, down-to-earth, with simple lyrics that people could relate to.

'I don't know how the public saw it, but I would carry little messages to them, give them little dance steps in the songs. It was a combination of dancing and the singing that we would present to them. Instead of going there and being the main attraction at these things, I would be the guy who presented it. And the public for me was always the main attraction, dancing in the aisles .... I always felt I was part of it with them, instead of leading them.'

As tremendous as the response may have seemed at that point, the best was yet to come. The impact of Haley's new approach to dance music had been limited to the influence of his records on radio and the jukebox, as well as the hotbed of regional interest that had swelled around Philadelphia, the South Jersey shore, and down through Delaware and Maryland as far as Baltimore.

The key to unleashing the full social power of this new music was through films. It was in that respect that Jim Myers made his most significant contribution to Haley's career. While many of Myers' claims are hotly contested by survivors of the era, the same people all give him the credit for getting 'Rock Around the Clock' onto the soundtrack of the controversial 1955 film *Blackboard Jungle*.

Blackboard Jungle dramatized the social change brought on by rock & roll in a violent and romantic story. The opening shot shows a group of kids in a schoolyard; the chain link fence surrounding the yard fills the foreground of the frame, symbolically placing these schoolkids in a jail. But at the same time 'Rock Around the Clock' is blaring off the soundtrack in a clarion call to break out of that jail and celebrate.

Blackboard Jungle contextualised rock & roll in a world of teenage violence and ignorance, an unfair categorization which did however provide a perfect opportunity for dramatizing a changing era. Early in the film Glenn Ford, who plays the dedicated teacher, tries to win over his class of juvenile delinquents by playing his collection of valuable jazz '78s in class. The kids respond by mocking him for listening to 'square' music and proceed to smash the precious records.

The overstatement of this imagery served to identify rock & roll as music of gangster rebellion and incipient communist infiltration in the minds of horrified adults. It also mythologized the music to the kids as their chance to express themselves in a medium clearly marked as their own province, and which furthermore offered a chance for imagined revenge against repressive parental and school authority. After all, this was the '50s, and the mantle of societal constraints hung uncomfortably over this era's teenagers, who reacted to cold war politics with the indifference of a generation that refused to go along with their parents' desire to relive the glory days of World War II.

A measure of how little Jim Myers understood the true significance of 'Rock Around the Clock' is shown by his explanation that he came up with the idea during World War II. 'The music came from the four years I spent overseas in the South Pacific in the army. There were Texans in my outfit. Many Texans are great fun people and they like to stomp their feet when they dance. Most of them can play the guitar and they have what they call a Texas swing beat that stuck in my head.

'We had a lot of Mexicans in the 32nd Infantry Division and they would sit by the campfires in the jungles and they would sing their beautiful Latin rhythms and chord progressions. And there was a black outfit that drove the trucks when we were back in a rest area, not in combat, I used to listen to them sing the spirituals. All these things sort of wove together to come up with the mould for "Rock Around the Clock".'

Nevertheless, it was Myers' singleminded determination to promote the song that resulted in its being selected for *Blackboard Jungle.* 'I sent 200 copies of the song to Hollywood,' he explains. When one of those copies ended up on the beginning of the film, *Blackboard Jungle* became the first movie to use a rock & roll theme song.

Decca reserviced 'Rock Around the Clock' to radio stations after the film was released and the record exploded, selling several million copies and suddenly turning Haley into one of the nation's top entertainment attractions. Virtually overnight Haley, Lord Jim and the others went from small time hustlers to moguls. In the space of a year they sold over six million records. On the Jersey shore in the summer of 1955 Haley and the Comets led the lives of Hollywood stars. Haley went out and bought five Cadillacs for the band. He bought a yacht, the *Comet,* and went on shark fishing expeditions in between lucrative gigs at the Steel Pier in Atlantic City and the Surf Club and the Starlight at Wildwood.

However, along with the success came a series of devastating personal tragedies that would haunt Haley throughout his life. In early 1955 his mother died and within a year, concurrent with Haley's rise to fame, his father and sister died horrible deaths from cancer and his fourth child became an infant cot death. 'I can remember him calling me on the phone,' recalls Dorothy Haley, 'and asking me did I think that this was God's way of making him pay for the wrongs that he had done, and I'd say I don't think God makes people pay that way.'

In late '55 the members of the band who were paid on a salary basis – drummer Dick Richards, bassist Marshall Lytle and saxophonist Joey Di'Ambrosia – left the Comets. Williamson and Grande were partners with Haley and did dramatically better than the others, who made $150.00 a week, as a result. The three left to form the Jodimars, who recorded several songs on Capitol supplied by Myers (his own 'Rattle My Bones' and Frank Pignatore's 'Clarabella') without much success.

Haley was forced to hire a new band quickly in order to make good on the booking commitments that were piling up in the wake of his new status. One of the new members, guitarist Frank Beecher, had been playing on the band's records for a year after replacing Danny Cedrone, who'd died of a heart attack in 1954. Al Rex agreed to rejoin his cronies on bass, and Rudy Pompilli, a highly acclaimed young saxophonist from Chester, joined up along with drummer Ralph Jones.

Beecher was an accomplished jazz guitarist when he joined the Comets for session work. During the 1940s he had worked in Buddy Greco's jazz band, then joined the Benny Goodman organization in 1948. 'When the Buddy Greco group broke up,' he explained, 'our rhythm section went with Benny Goodman. We auditioned for the job and we were accepted.'

Charlie Christian had been Beecher's idol at the time, so when his stint with Goodman turned out to be a very stale musical experience Beecher left. With Goodman he had 'no liberty whatsoever, except for some things that were inserted at my request. I came back home quite disgusted.'

Beecher returned to the Philadelphia area, got a day job and woodshedded at night with a three piece lounge group, the Larry Wayne Trio, which consisted of accordion, bass and guitar. Haley gave him a call to play with the Comets and Beecher showed up for the session that produced 'Happy Baby'. Haley probably wasn't ready for Beecher's advanced ideas of guitar accompaniment. 'We came to an ad-lib guitar solo,' says Beecher, 'and I started playing with a jazz feel. I played the first four bars and everything came to a halt. Haley said he'd never sell any records if I played like that. I had to stick to major scales.'

Despite Haley's admonition, Beecher's playing on 'Happy Baby' was remarkable. He phrased beautiful runs behind the vocal chorus in the intro, used augmented jazz chords as fills in his rhythm accompaniment and swung a breathtaking through-the-scale solo. His playing was more fluid and melodically inventive than Cedrone's had been, yet he was unaware there was anything special about it.

'It was just another job, really,' he recalls. 'Just a recording session. I never stopped to think about it. It just didn't mean anything to me. I wasn't impressed with it – it was just another job to play. I came out of the jazz field in the '40s, I wasn't playing rock & roll, I wanted to play like Charlie Christian, so I had to change my style. They wanted to play a more basic style than I was used to, more country really, they called it rockabilly. But I got to put some advanced technical stuff in here and there.'

Beecher had been working with the Comets in the studio for about a year before Haley hired him permanently. 'He asked me if I would be interested in going on the road if he needed a lead guitar player,' says Beecher. 'I said I would if the money was right, if the situation was right I'd think about it.'

Nine: Calling All Comets

WHILE HALEY WAS up in the hills outside of Chester learning to be a singing cowboy, another scene was developing in downtown Chester that had no apparent connection, but would later figure in Haley's career. In Chester's Eighth ward, a poor community where Italian, Irish and Polish immigrants lived in two and three story brick houses, a young Italian saxophone player named Rudy Pompilli was building a reputation as a powerful musician.

Pompilli grew up at 3rd and Broomall streets in Chester, and studied, he later recalled, in 'a crowded room with Professor Carlo Musemeci and his students, Sod Vacarro, Nick Mancini, Sam Poliafico, Nick Casamassi, Joe Valzone, Pooch Yanelli – all getting our fingers cracked when we goofed.'

Rudy was well liked around Chester, but was so intent on practicing and playing that he didn't socialize that much beyond his musical confines. His horn was his world, and people who knew Rudy back then all recall how loudly he played. 'There was no one like him,' says a patron of the Nite Cap lounge, where Pompilli played regularly during his later years. 'I never heard a saxophone played so loud and hard.'

Pompilli's jam sessions were legendary. He'd play with a trio backing up a stripper at Andy's musical bar at 3rd and Palmer and blow the roof off the place. The jam sessions at Mazza's, on 3rd and Penn in Chester, would last until the early morning hours, before the musicians and their friends repaired to Bowie's all night diner for breakfast.

Pompilli's reputation earned him a call with the Ralph Martieri orchestra, where his flashy playing and showmanship brought him to the attention of the jazz public. Pompilli was voted best new saxophonist in *Downbeat*'s 1953 jazz poll.

61

Martieri's outfit recorded a popular local version of Haley's hit 'Crazy Man, Crazy,' and Pompilli developed a showstopping theatrical device – he'd play a solo and slowly arch his back, lowering himself to the floor as he played until he was blowing the horn while lying flat on his back.

Rudy also played in a Chester group called the Merry Men along with drummer Ralph Jones and a couple of other local musicians. They played over the air at WPWA, which is where they first met Haley. 'We would finish our little jazz show,' Jones recalls, 'and he would come on and do a country and western show. I got to know him that way. Bill used to sweep out the station, he was a hanger-on there, really. He had a Dr. Soltz commercial, the dentist downtown, that he used to do. Somedays he'd be on the air by himself, just guitar. I used to hear him, he was very good, he was actually an excellent country and western singer. He was a champion yodeller, too.

'Rudy and I played together for twenty years,' says Jones. 'We were with a group called Little Arnie's Four Horsemen. That was a comedy act. We had two comedians—the accordionist, Little Arnie, was a comedian and so was the bass player, but they were both excellent musicians.'

When Haley put together the new Comets, Pompilli filled the saxophone position immediately, but Jones didn't join the band at the same time. Haley had already asked Jones to play with him earlier and Jones had turned down the offer.

'He was playing up at Broomall Cafe and he called me,' Jones explains. 'I was working as a milkman believe it or not. I was just playing weekends and weddings and things like that. Dick Richards had left and a fellow named Dean Tinker was playing drums with him up at the Broomall. He called me to join and I turned him down. I didn't like the music, I was playing jazz and I didn't dig it at all.'

Once Pompilli was in the band he kept after Haley to hire Jones. With Haley's newfound celebrity status, Jones was definitely more interested the second time around. 'Bill called me from Ohio and said he'd like me to join the act,' Jones says. 'I said OK. It was that simple.'

The first great rock & roll band was complete.

'We were the first big rock & roll group, no question about that,' points out Jones. 'When I joined they already had the style worked out.' The group that the defecting Jodimars had been part of was as much a hillbilly band as a rock & roll band; drums and sax had been added as an afterthought to what was in essence the Saddlemen line-up. Even though this band had played gigs promoting hits with guitar solos like 'Rock the Joint' and 'Rock Around the Clock' there hadn't even been a guitarist in the band – Billy Williamson played the leads on steel guitar. The Frank Beecher/Rudy Pompilli/Ralph Jones Comets were the first band assembled to play that kind of music and during their five years together they cut some excellent records.

This version of the Comets established many of the conventions of rock & roll performance and presentation that would become standard practice over the years. Haley's approach to the stage shows was pretty sophisticated for the time. Unlike most early rock presentations, which emphasized a single front-man personality backed by anonymous, if talented, support musicians, Haley spread the spotlight out among the other members of his group.

Haley may have been the focal point, but the Comets were the show. Haley hardly moved from the spot where he was rooted to the stage, but Al Rex would throw his giant bass fiddle up in the air, then jump onto its side while still playing it. Rudy Pompilli would do his back breaking acrobatics with the saxophone, and the others would jive and joke accordingly.

The set was air tight, with a number of comic interludes to promote the pace. 'We used the same pattern all the time,' explains Al Rex. 'Haley would do his own stuff. He would open up with maybe two tunes, then he would throw in "Rudy's Rock" where I used to kill myself on the bass. And Rudy used to squash me when he used to sit on my back. I'm telling you he used to laugh like a son of a bitch. I felt like my guts were gonna come out. Then I'd have to throw it up in the air and stand on it so here I am puffed, right? I'm winded, I mean it, sweating like a pig and all of a sudden Haley throws the guitar at me and says 'C'mon Duke, come up here and sing.

'He used to get me up to the microphone right after I'd knock myself out on the bass fiddle, throwing it all through the air and I couldn't even breathe. You'd think let's do something else and give the guy a chance to catch his breath. One day I went up and I start tearing the place apart and he kept saying "Do another one, do another one," and I kept doing another number. All I used to do was three numbers in the show, but that time he had me do six or seven. I'd sing "Flip, Flop Fly," "Tutti Frutti," "Long Tall Sally," I used to do "Hound Dog," Haley would get mad at me if I'd do that. This was even before Presley did it, Haley didn't like these guys from Philadelphia that wrote the song.'

One of the routines Al Rex became notorious for involved splitting his trousers during his slapstick escapades with the bass. Like a lot of good bits, this one started out as an accident. 'You know how that happened?' he asks. 'We were playing in Philadelphia and we used to wear the tight tuxedos y'know. So this one night I go to lay down on my back and kick up the bass and my pants split because I used to sweat a lot and everybody started laughing and hollering at me. So Billy Williamson told me I should put a patch on my tuxedo and work the routine into the act. So on special occasions I used to wear these tuxedos with a patch in the crotch so when I would lay down and kick up the bass everybody would say "Jesus Christ! Look! His pants are splitting!" '

Williamson had to cue a lot of the comic routines because Haley was the straight man in the Comets, just as he was in previous performing units. 'Billy was the brains of the outfit,' says Ralph Jones. 'He was the ideas man.' Williamson did a little of his own singing, with Rex and Pompilli joining in for an occasional trio. 'Billy would crack a couple of jokes,' says Rex, 'but you see the way our performances ran we didn't want any slow spots, everything was fast man, go-go-go. Once in a while Billy would come up and say "Jeez, we got a telegram here for Al Rex. It says 'Man, you're great, you're great' and it's signed 'Al Rex's mother.' " Then we'd go right into a number.'

Beecher didn't escape these Marx Brothers routines, either. 'I did a comedy routine,' he recalls. 'I used to sing a song in a high-pitched voice imitating a little child three or four years old. I would insert different remarks, like in "You Made Me Love You" I used to sing in one part "you dirty rat". In another part I'd change my voice to a low voice. I got quite a response from that. Bill would build me up when he introduced me as one of the best baritones in the world and how I'd sung here and there, he'd get all the people keyed up. Everyone was wondering what it's

64

"MY SWEET LITTLE GIRL FROM NEVADA"

Words and Music by
GUS BRAUN, CHARLIE REBER and HARRY DAVIS

A 1950 sheet music cover featuring a small photo of Haley
and a Cowboy Records label crediting "Bill Haley on Vocal."

The Four Aces of Western Swing. *Above, left to right:* 'Smiling' Al Constantine, Tex King, Bill Haley, 'Bashful' Barney Barnard. *Below:* Haley and the Four Aces of Western Swing promoting their single 'Candy Kisses'/'Tennessee Border' *Rex Zario Collection*

Yodelling Bill Haley. *Rex Zario Collection*

Haley and Jack Howard in the first rock & roll riot. *Rex Zario Collection*

Bill Haley and his Comets. *Clockwise:* Bill Haley, Billy Williamson, Rudy Pompilli, Frank Beecher, Johnny Grande, Al Rex, Ralph Jones. *Decca Records*

Above: Haley at his beach music headquarters in Wildwood, New Jersey. *Below:* Ralph Jones and Bill Haley. *Rex Zario Collection*

A rare shot of Haley during a Decca recording session. *Rex Zario Collection*

Haley and the Comets on the set of *Don't Knock the Rock. Columbia Pictures*

all about and he's telling them how deep my voice is and how great I am, then I'd walk up to the microphone and they'd give this introduction, like the Ink Spots, but instead of coming in with this deep voice I'd come in with this very high pitched voice and they used to just scream. It was a big shock.'

The horsing around was just window dressing for the band's main feature, big beat dance music. The band was the loudest by far of its time, a fact that irritated some of the people at Decca who went to see them only to complain that Haley's vocals were drowned by the din. Beecher had technical problems at first because of the volume. 'When I started,' he says, 'I used my own guitar, an Epiphone, and at the volume we had to play I just couldn't do it. The feedback was tremendous.'

Beecher went out and got a Gibson Les Paul, which was well suited to the high intensity sound the band generated, and top lead guitarists ever since have sworn by the instrument. Beecher's live playing defined the guitar soloist's role – in fact it wasn't for another decade, when guitarists like Alvin Lee in the aptly named Ten Years After would reproduce Beecher solos note-for-note, that a lot of his ideas were brought into common use. One of the act's high points was Beecher's guitar solo spot.

'I did a guitar solo,' he explains, 'they call it the guitar boogie but it wasn't copied from a record or anything. It was just something I put together. I'd play a fast boogie woogie pattern and the band would play background. It was pretty exciting, the kids would go nuts. It was put together to be exciting. I would jump around as I played and move with the music a little bit.'

Sometimes the action got so hot and heavy that instruments broke, and the band would recover with a piece of stagemanship worthy of one of their more pyrotechnical progeny, the Who. 'Haley used to break up guitars,' muses Beecher. 'He used L-7's which he'd drop. He broke up a couple of basses too. One time the bass player slipped off and fell. The bass went flying, the neck flew off, the back flew off. Luckily he didn't hurt himself. He ran out and picked up the neck and held it in the air with the strings hanging down. The audience thought it was all in the act. He almost broke his neck.'

Without fail, every show would end with 'Rock Around the Clock,' the song guaranteed to leave the audience whipped up to a fever pitch. 'Every artist has one tune,' Haley later explained, 'and that was my tune. I carried it with me in my back pocket, and I used it all the time. It was a natural. You're talking about *the* tune of rock and roll.'

Haley's live show tore the house down wherever it went, and according to an interview Bill did years later with Ken Terry, strongly influenced a young singer named Elvis Presley. 'Colonel Tom Parker wasn't Presley's manager at the time,' Haley explained. 'As I recall, Presley was then being managed by somebody out of Memphis. And Elvis was just another kid with a guitar. But around this time, Colonel Tom Parker became interested, because Elvis had had three or four small records, and was playing around through the South and Colonel Tom Parker called Lord Jim Ferguson, my manager, and he said, "Look, I've got this kid, I can take him over, but I want him to get some experience, would you let me take him on tour with Bill?" And since my manager and Tom were good friends, he said, "Yeah". And as I recall, the tour was Hank Snow and myself and the first show was in Omaha, Nebraska. It was a regular one-nighter tour. And I remember Presley came on the show. He was a big tall young kid. He didn't have too much personality at that time, I remember. He went on the show, and the first two nights I didn't even catch his act. I think Hank Snow went on first, half an hour or so, and then we went on. We closed the show naturally. The first time I remember talking to Elvis was in, I think, Oklahoma City. He was standing backstage and we were getting ready to go on. And he came over and told me he was a fan of mine and we talked – an awful nice kid. Contrary to everything that's been written about him, he was a nice guy. And he wanted to learn, which was the important thing. At that time, he was willing to listen.

'I remember one night he went out and did a show and asked me what I thought. I had watched the show and I told him, "Elvis, you're leaning too much on ballads and what have you. You've got a natural rhythm feeling, so do your rhythm tunes." Now this was a long time before he was a big hit, you know. (I think he was doing a tune called "That's All Right, Mama," or something at the time.) So he went out and he had the attitude which most young kids do that he was really going to go out there and stop the show and knock Bill Haley off the stage, which at that time was an impossibility because we were number one and what have you. And he went out and he was facing Bill Haley fans. You have to realize, it's like you go up against Bruce (i.e., Peter) Frampton right now with some kid from Memphis, he's not going to do it. And when he came off after doing his show – he was accepted, you know – and when I came back after doing my show he was kinda half crying in the dressing room, very downhearted and I sat down with him and I told him, "Look, you got a lot of talent", and I explained to him a lot of things. He and I buddied together for about a week and a half after that, and I didn't realize, of course, that Elvis was going to be *Elvis,* and he left and we finished the tour and went on. From time to time for about six months we'd see one of his records reviewed and so on. And I went to Cleveland to Bill Randall, who was the top disc jockey in Cleveland at that time on WERE, and I started telling him how good Elvis was and how much I liked the kid. And of course at that time Colonel Tom was trying to get him started. So anyway, Randall had some connections – I'm not too sure of this part of the story – and Elvis went in and did his shows with Bill and what have you and the next thing Elvis got his break. The Colonel got him his deal with RCA and so on.'

Haley also recalled meeting Buddy Holly around the same time. 'I met Buddy when he was still starting in Lubbock, Texas. I was doing a one-nighter tour and driving over to Lubbock – I was appearing that night at some auditorium there – and we had a flat tire on the way in on the other car. I got there first, just my manager and I, and the stadium was full and, you know, there was the usual pandemonium and the promoter going crazy. Finally he came to me and said "Bill, you got to go on." I said, "Well, how can I go on? I don't have any instruments or band or anything." So he said "Well, I got a couple of kids here that will go it alone with you." And he introduced me to Buddy Holly and the Crickets. This was before they made records or anything. And we went out and we did probably half an hour before my band got there.

'I didn't see Buddy – he was very good – for a long time after that. The next time I saw Buddy Holly I was in the Decca offices in New York City, and of course Coral Records had the same offices and the same company. And here I meet Buddy and the Crickets and they had a hit at the time, and we had a big reunion. The next time I saw him was in Jacksonville, Florida. He was on the show with a group called the Teen Tops ("Short Shorts"), Jerry Lee Lewis and myself, and we had three days together there and became closer friends.

'He was a nice quiet kid; he was very sociable. Buddy was very friendly, you know. "Come over to my dressing room and I'll come over to yours, let's listen to each other's songs." The tragic part of that story was we were on a one-nighter tour – I forget where it was the night he got killed – but I was due in the next night. I had hoped to see him and I didn't get to see him.'

Ten: Rock & Roll Gets the Blame

As 1955 ENDED rock & roll had become a household word and Haley and the Comets were its best-known practitioners. Haley would continue to pace the music's popularity in the U.S. during the following year. At that point he was still a highly respected musician – he was voted Rhythm and Blues Personality of the Year by *Downbeat* magazine's readers, scoring over Joe Williams, Joe Turner, Dinah Washington and Ruth Brown.

The new Comets had made a series of particularly strong recordings, beginning with 'R.O.C.K.', a celebration of the music and their place in it. Haley gives a brief nonsense definition of rock, then traces musical history from Strauss waltzes to W. C. Handy blues, concluding 'Then Haley came along with a rockin' song' to which the band choruses 'Crazy Man, Crazy'. The flip side 'Rock-a-Beatin'-Boogie' was pretty much the same idea, with a great call-and-response pattern between sax and guitar that breaks to an excellent Beecher solo.

Pompilli's influence on the Comets came through dramatically on the next record, 'The Saints Rock 'N' Roll', which used Rudy's hot blues riffs more thoroughly in the arrangement than ever. Sax was pretty much a gimmick sound in the band before that, but Pompilli blew an incredibly hot chorus solo. Guitar, drums and bass also all traded solos before the irresistibly hot-riffing finale.

It was 'See You Later Alligator' that cemented Haley's reputation with the public. The record, which opens with Beecher's high-pitched stage voice saying the phrase, was probably the best example of the familiar phrase formula at work. The record sold a million copies in a single month and people who wouldn't admit to being rock & roll fans found themselves answering 'After a while crocodile'.

Milt Gabler had heard a regional hit version of 'See You Later Alligator' and recognized the connection right away. 'It was one of those things where he decided to go up and record it just that quick,' recalls Ralph Jones. Jones hadn't played on any Comets records up until that point because Gabler had been using a session drummer, Billy Guesack. 'This was sort of a kick in the ass to me,' says Jones, 'being out playing with a group and not being able to record. Haley said he was using Guesack and he didn't want to change a successful formula. He said it had nothing to do with my playing but that didn't make sense to me. So I complained to Johnny and Billy, I said "What the hell I'm out here doing the job, why can't I play on the records?" So then "See You Later Alligator" came along. We were covering somebody else who had it out and it was going like crazy in the midwest.

'I think the week before we were playing at a nightclub in New Jersey and Guesack came over to hear me. He said to Bill "I see no reason why this boy can't play on your records." So Bill said to Johnny "We're gonna give Jonesy a shot, see what happens." Well I knew what Guesack did — he kept his snare extremely tight — and how he played it — it was easy, it was simple, really.

'So we were in the studio and Milt Gabler was in the control booth, saying "Lemme hear that drum," y'know. Before anybody else, "Lemme hear that rim-shot!" So I let him hear a few, he was satisfied.'

Gabler laughs when he recalls 'See You Later Alligator'. 'It was covering a record, and Haley hadn't heard it until he came into the studio. I had the record in my office, which was on the 15th floor, and it was on the weekend. I wanted to play the record for him and I couldn't get in my office so I borrowed a hammer from the super and broke the glass on my office door to open the lock from the inside.'

In the space of one week in March of 1956 Bill Haley and the Comets recorded some of their finest work. The first of three sessions during that time, on 23rd March, yielded the instrumental masterpiece 'Rudy's Rock', which was the high point of the *Rock Around the Clock* film. The song is a hard driving vehicle for the best extended blowing session Pompilli got with the Comets. He shows real melodic imagination in his playing, and the tom-tom handclap rhythm pattern he solos over is one of the most exciting moments in the band's history. Few contemporary horn players could match Rudy on this kind of material, and it's a shame he didn't get to do more of it.

'Goofin' Around' is one long, tremendous guitar solo from Frank Beecher phrased over a spirited backing track. Beecher stops only once during the tune to let Al Rex slap out a bass solo before the guitar takes over again in a climactic run which ends up referencing Chuck Berry 'Hide and Seek' reworked the popular song 'The Hucklebuck cleverly, with an excellent r & b style vocal by Billy Williamson and good solos from Pompilli and Beecher. 'Hey Then, There Now' is a vocal trio tune with accordion backing very similar to some of the western swing numbers done by the Saddlemen. 'Tonight's the Night,' which features beautiful guitar accompaniment throughout, is notable for the dual guitar-saxophone solo and a sophisticated arrangement that utilizes the jazz background of some of the players. "Hook, Line and Sinker' is a throwaway novelty tune distinguished only by good guitar and sax solos.

Four days later the band did it again. 'Blue Comet Blues' is a flat-out rocker, again with a touch of Berry in Beecher's intro, which goes on to explore the possibilities of a blues guitar solo in a rock context, one more forceful example of how far ahead of other rock guitarists Frank Beecher was both as a theorist and a virtuoso player. 'Calling All Comets', another Pompilli triumph, opens with a clarion saxophone bleating its irresistible call to the dance floor before breaking to a beautifully arranged main theme reminiscent of the Louis Jordan sound. The body of the tune is brilliantly simple, laying a stock rhythmic figure played by the guitar over the slap-back bass and driving drum pattern, with Pompilli soloing over that. As the song builds the band starts playing up the scale and Williamson adds the steel guitar 'lightning flashes' for dramatic effect. 'Choo Choo Ch' Boogie' is a great song, done here with Louis Jordan's version in mind although the rhythm track is obviously rockified.

Three days later they recorded 'Hot Dog Buddy Buddy', a fine example of Haley's hit concept when it worked. The band is at its best, with Jones' drumming particularly on the money. Haley's voice actually cracks from the strain as he screams the title. The lyrics are about fighting, which is interesting in light of the fact that Haley kept saying that fighting had nothing to do with the music. Another great riffing chorus features Beecher in one of his flying-fingers solos.

The last songs from these sessions are less interesting. 'A Rockin' Little Tune', with its prominent accordion part, seems inappropriately titled, although Beecher and Pompilli, who often worked miracles with bad material, played brilliant solos. 'Rockin' Through the Rye' is the first of Haley's series of unfortunate adaptions of rock & roll to folk tunes from other countries. The idea is forced, but as soon as Rudy's solo begins the song takes off.

Another film, *Rock Around the Clock*, further enhanced the reputation of Haley and the Comets. '1956 was the biggest year,' recalls Ralph Jones. 'Everything busted open for us, the movies, the tours, everything.' *Rock Around the Clock*, a glib rags-to-riches story built around a fairytale account of Haley's rise to the top, was B-movie producer Sam Katzman's attempt to cash in on rock & roll's popularity for Columbia studios. 'Our booking agent, Jolly Joyce, knew Katzman,' explained Ralph Jones. 'Katzman's son said "Hey, you gotta get Bill Haley and do a movie." Simple as all that.'

Katzman had created a monster. Soon the rival studios were turning out their own versions of these film vehicles for rock & roll. *Rock Around the Clock* featured nine of Haley's best tunes – the title track, 'R-O-C-K', 'Mambo Rock', 'Razzle Dazzle', 'See You Later Alligator', 'ABC Boogie', 'Happy Baby', 'Rudy's Rock', and 'Rock-a-Beatin' Boogie'. The film also presented the Platters singing 'Only You' and 'The Great Pretender'.

In the film the reason Haley and the Comets become popular is that everywhere they go the local kids love them. In the cinema the excited, happily dancing audiences involved the theatergoing kids in the action vicariously and turned the shows into live concerts, sometimes to the displeasure of local authorities, who banned the film in several instances.

The *Rock Around the Clock* ban was part of a growing backlash against rock & roll mounted by authorities who were alternately confused, angered and frightened by the phenomenon. The 28th March 1956 edition of *The New York Times* carried a story from Hartford, Connecticut, headlined 'Rock & Roll Called "Communicable Disease".' A psychiatrist named Francis J. Braceland termed it a 'cannibalistic and tribalistic' sort of music. 'It is insecurity and rebellion,' he said, 'that impels teenagers to wear "ducktail" haircuts, wear zoot suits and carry on boisterously at rock & roll affairs.' The psychiatrist was commenting on a rock riot that saw 100 fans thrown out of a local theater.

Racial tension in the United States was particularly acute at that time in the wake of the landmark Supreme Court decision of 1954 outlawing the 'separate-but-equal' policy of racial segregation in the country. Anti-segregationists, particularly in the South, saw rock & roll as a plot to infiltrate colored music into the minds of white teenagers. Asa Carter, executive secretary of the Alabama White Citizens Committee, charged that the National Association for the Advancement of Colored People (NAACP) was behind the plot. Carter described rock & roll as the "basic heavy beat of the Negroes. It appeals to the base in man, it brings out animalism and vulgarity'.

Carter went on to ask juke box operators to destroy 'immoral' records in the new rhythm, but distributors said this would mean eliminating most of their hits. Mr Carter suggested other black records should be banned too. Roy Wilkins of the NAACP responded 'Some people in the South are blaming us for everything from measles to atomic fall outs.'

Haley found himself a spokesman for rock & roll as a positive force. 'Rock and roll does help to combat racial discrimination,' he said at the time. 'We have performed to mixed groups all over the country and have watched the kids sit side by side just enjoying the music while being entertained by white and negro performers sharing the same stage.

'Despite what people might think, a lot of blood, sweat, pain, trouble, work and worry goes into all of our music. We aim our material at the teenagers because we want them to accept it, and we always try to give the people what they want. We will continue to keep doing good shows and continue to cut lyrically clean records with good danceable beats.'

Nevertheless, the storm of criticism continued. Rock & roll records were banned from swimming pool juke boxes in San Antonio, Texas, by the city council, which explained that 'Its primitive beat attracted undesirable elements given to practicing their spastic gyrations in abbreviated bathing suits.'

Roosevelt University sociologist S. Kirson Weinberg saw

rock & roll as a manifestation of the insecurities of the age. 'The effect of the music,' he pointed out, 'is more predominant in girls.'

Band leader Meredith Wilson branded rock & roll as 'the music of idiots,' adding 'rock & roll is dull, ugly, amateurish, immature, trite, banal and stale. It glorifies the mediocre, the nasty, the bawdy, the cheap, the tasteless.' He went on to make the hilarious suggestion that Mitch Miller was responsible for rock & roll. 'The beard did it,' he fumed.

An ominous note was sounded at a House of Representatives antitrust subcommittee meeting when entertainer Billy Rose slammed BMI for promoting rock & roll. A few years later disc jockey/promoter Alan Freed would be ruined in the payola scandal.

'I don't see,' said Rose, 'how it [BMI] can escape the charge that it is responsible for rock & roll and other musical monstrosities which are muddying up the air waves.' Rose spoke of travels to communist countries where he heard Soviet orchestras play songs he hadn't heard in a long time rather than rock & roll. 'In other words our best musical talents seemed to be having an easier time crashing through the Iron Curtain than through the electronic curtain which the broadcasting companies have set up through their three way control of airwaves, the outfits which publish [music] and the companies which make phonograph records.'

Variety, the show business trade magazine, kept track of rock's growing box office success (*Rock 'N' Roll B.O. Dynamite* blared the April 11, 1956 cover headline), but was openly skeptical of its merits:

> Rock 'n' roll – the most explosive show biz phenomenon of the decade – may be getting too hot to handle. While its money-making potential has made it all but irresistible, its Svengali grip on the teenagers   produced a staggering wave of juvenile violence and mayhem . . .
>
> On the police blotters, rock 'n' roll has also been writing an unprecedented record. In one locale after another, rock 'n' roll shows, or disc hops where such tunes have been played, have touched off every type of juvenile delinquency.

The story goes on to detail damage resulting from Alan Freed's Brooklyn Paramount concert, warn that theaters might cancel rock shows for fear of damage, describe the switch from rock & roll to 'Theater of Beautiful Music' by Boston's WMEX, claim that rock & roll's popularity is already flagging anyway, and report on an account from the *Minneapolis Star* about a local rock & roll promotion:

Intended as a teenagers' rock 'n' roll party, the affair came a cropper when part of the audience, including children 12 and 13 years old and even younger, staged a near riot . . .

Police said that while rock & roll records were played on the stage, the youngsters danced and whooped it up in the aisles and floor space down front. When ordered to return to their seats, there was a lusty chorus of boos aimed at the squad of police that had been summoned. A hurled beer can narrowly missed hitting one policeman.

A party started when three radio station staff members, gaudily attired and wearing scotch plaid caps, gestured and shouted to pep up the audience as the records played. On the stage a 'panel' of teenage fans selected the records and the audience's response was supposed to determine whether they were 'hits' or 'misses'. There weren't many of the latter.

A small 'riot' at a Haley concert in Atlanta merited extensive coverage in *Variety* of 30th May:

Five teenage boys were arrested as a result of fights at a rock 'n' roll concert at Ponce de Leon Park, baseball home of the Atlanta Crackers, where 10,000 gathered for a show headed by Bill Haley & His Comets Thursday night. Another teenage boy was hit in the head by a flying beer bottle.

Police reported they arrested the five youths in separate incidents. Spectators said it was hard to figure out who was doing the fighting and who was dancing in the aisles.

Only a few weeks later, *Newsweek* ran an account of another disturbance at a Haley concert:

Even before the joint began to jump there was trouble at the National Guard Armory in Washington, D.C. 5,000 people, mostly teenagers, poured in for some rock 'n' roll. Knives flashed and one young man was cut in the arm. Inside 25 special officers waited for Bill Haley & the Comets to swing into the big beat.

The story went on to describe how as the band started to play the crowd began dancing in the aisles, only to be chased back to their seats by the cops. Then, the audience flipped out when Haley and the boys broke into 'Hot Dog, Buddy, Buddy'. Some of the kids danced and some scuffled. William Warfield, a seventeen-year-old high school junior, suffered a severe cut over one eye and was rushed to the hospital, where he was diagnosed as having a brain concussion. 'Before I knew it,' he said, 'everyone was pounding everybody.'

The fighting spilled out into the street, where a nineteen-year-old was struck on the head and a sixteen-year-old was cut on the ear. Two cars were stoned and somebody turned in a false alarm. 'It's that jungle strain that gets them all worked up,' complained armory manager Arthur 'Dutch' Bergman.

In San Jose, California, one of the biggest rock & roll riots caused another wave of protest against the music. The fans routed seventy-three policemen, injuring eleven people and causing $3,000 worth of damage. Santa Cruz promptly banned concerts. On the east coast, a concert at Asbury Park's Convention Hall on 30th June erupted into a brawl among the 2,700 participants, leaving twenty-five hospitalized. Asbury Park's mayor banned future rock & roll shows, which prompted Jersey City mayor Bernard J. Berry and city commissioners Lawrence A. Whipple and Joshua Ringle to cancel a planned 'Rock and Roll under the Stars Concert' led by Haley. Promoter Ed Otto and master of ceremonies Paul Whiteman of big band fame tried desperately to clear the concert site, Roosevelt Stadium, for use. 'We were executed by remote control,' complained Otto, while Whiteman maintained the show would not be violent. 'It was to be a concert,' he said.

In Pittsburgh, another disturbance led to more official censure. After eight teenagers were arrested outside a concert which featured Carl Perkins, Al Hibbler and Illinois Jacquet, The Pennsylvania Chiefs of Police Association, which was meeting in Pittsburgh at the time, labelled rock & roll 'an incentive to teenage unrest.' Pittsburgh inspector Fred Good said police 'did not pretend to be music critics or have a technical understanding of beat and rhythms,' but said 'nevertheless, wherever there's been teenage trouble lately, rock & roll has almost always been in the background. The songs are more suggestive than those sung in burlesque houses and the rhythm seems to have some special hypnotic effect which has created ridiculous male hootchie-kootchie dancers.'

Haley's response to these charges was to record a song defending the rock & roll generation called 'Teenager's Mother'. Lyrically the tune was painfully awkward for Haley to sing, but it is the first message song in rock & roll history. Haley tells the mothers that rock & roll is 'all your Johnny had' and that when those mothers were kids they had their own kind of fun with the Charleston (at which point the Comets adapt a little 'Charleston' chorus that sounds surprisingly good).

'At the time that the kids are out listening to music,' Haley argued, 'they're not getting into trouble. When they're home listening to records, they're not getting into mischief. It can only help them, not hurt them. A lot depends on the parents and how they take care of their children, and a lot depends on the entertainers. Bad lyrics can have an effect on teenagers. I have always been careful not to use suggestive lyrics.

'Usually I try to use expressions that the kids can easily remember and repeat. For instance, my newest record is called 'Hot Dog, Buddy, Buddy'. It's an expression that the kids have used to me in expressing their approval of something we have done.'

When Haley described his responsibilities as an entertainer you can sense that he was comparing himself to Elvis Presley, whose hip-shaking gyrations were starting to cause quite a stir. 'A lot depends on the entertainer and how he controls the crowd,' Haley said. 'The music is stimulating enough without creating additional excitement.'

Most of Haley's attention, though, was directed at other musicians who were criticizing rock & roll. 'Wherever we appear the public has come out in droves, yet the industry is tearing the music down. If rock & roll can bring people into the ballrooms and make them dance, why then don't those musicians who call rock & roll *bad* music write their own arrangements against the beat and form small units of, say, nine men? I know for a fact that a lot of the musicians who think my music is bad are not working steadily. If the music is bad, as they contend, what's to stop them from making it good by writing their own arrangements?'

Haley was making an excellent point with this argument, but

he hardly realized at the time that he'd be faced with the same problem before too long.

For the time being, of course, he was riding high. Haley and the Comets headlined the first full scale rock & roll touring show, an extravaganza assembled by the current Ringling Brothers and Barnum and Bailey Circus mastermind, Irving Feld. The package also included the Platters and Frankie Lymon and the Teenagers and hit major cities all across the United States and Canada.

'This act got along very well,' recalls Ralph Jones. 'There were never any problems. Bill was the leader, nobody disputed that.'

Haley and the Comets travelled in style. 'It started out that we used to use five Cadillacs to go to our shows,' Jones says, 'but that got to be a bit too much. So Bill hired this bus driver and this bus to go out to Ohio one time and he couldn't believe the bus kept up with him so he bought the bus and hired the driver. We sent it back home and had it all fixed up.'

The second Bill Haley and the Comets feature film, *Don't Knock the Rock*, was made during 1956 and took the anti-rock & roll factions head on. The film was actually a morality play made to show that rock & roll was a positive force in teenage life that was being sabotaged by unscrupulous elements. The action of the script followed the political fallout from rock & roll in '56 pretty closely. After dances were banned in one town, the daughter of a local politician brought liquor to another function in order to deliberately discredit the event.

The most bizarre feature of the film came when Haley and Alan Freed cooked up a 'play' that demonstrated how rock & roll paralleled such dance explosions of the past as the Charleston and the waltz, and equated the parents' outrage against rock & roll with their parents' hostility for dance forms of the past. The lesson may seem forced in retrospect but at the time the film was released it was pretty topical stuff.

Haley got a large enough part in the film to come off looking painfully square, especially when he tried to interject hip patter into a conversation. His lines weren't the best, of course – at one point the script-writers put an incredibly awkward sentence into his mouth which likened freedom of the press to a complimentary dry cleaning service.

However, as far as the presentation of the music went, *Don't Knock the Rock* was a triumph. The basement setting where the band played the sublime 'Calling All Comets' provided a visual cliche of underground rock that anticipated the Beatles' early use of the concept as well as its proliferation recently as a punk rock setting. The film also included Haley's version of 'Rip It Up' and Little Richard playing 'Tutti Frutti' and 'Long Tall Sally'.

Eleven: Rocking Around the World

OVER THE 1956 Christmas holidays Bill Haley threw a big party at his custom-built house near Booth Corners. Haley was extremely proud of the house, which was designed by a friend to incorporate all the latest features of '50s luxury living. He called the sprawling ranch house Melody Manor. It was built on a plot of several heavily wooded acres of land facing Faulk Road. At the edge of the property stood the tiny house Haley's family had lived in, right next to the one-room schoolhouse where Haley used to bring his guitar to school and yodel for his classmates.

'He built it for his mother,' said Milt Gabler of Haley's house. 'But the funny part about the whole property was the chicken shack in front of the house. If I had a chicken coop it would be in the back of the house. Here's this nice low brick house with a den down below, it was a fairly new house, he said he built it for his mother, and at that point they had not moved the chicken shack. Here you go to see this big star and he's got chicken in the front.'

Haley's determination to build the dream house symbolic of his success on the very ground where he nurtured his early dreams of stardom shows how deeply he was tied to his family memories. But Melody Manor became a tombstone to his family when the last of his living relatives suddenly died. His sister was only thirty-five when she died, while his cancer-ravaged father suffered a horrible death in which 'he threw up his lungs'.

'When his father died it left its mark on him,' says Frank Beecher.

Haley compensated for the loss of his family with a burning devotion to his second wife and their children. He was determined to make Melody Manor a place of love and merriment, and he would throw lavish parties for family, friends and

80

relatives. He built a series of maze-like sidewalks through the woods around the property for his kids to roller skate on. At the beginning of the sidewalk where it joins the driveway in front of the barn-sized garage where Haley housed his Cadillacs you can still read his second wife's name scrawled into the cement to this day.

Scattered across the grounds were a number of massive barbecues for the outdoor summer parties, but it was the Christmas party that Haley was particularly fond of. 'We used to have a huge Christmas party every year out at Bill's house,' recalls Ralph Jones. 'He would never be away from home at Christmas time. I remember one year he turned Dinah Shore down to be on her show at Christmas for some damn good money.'

The '56 party was highlighted by an elaborate color home movie travelogue covering the band's exploits during the year, particularly of their travels with the massive Irving Feld 'Galaxy of the Stars' tour. 'We used to make up these films we'd taken on the road,' explained Jones, 'to show our wives what we did on the road. It was a fun thing.'

It must have been a sight – Melody Manor festooned with Christmas decorations, all the Cadillacs in the snow, the lavish spread in the basement den, records by the band playing on the portable Decca machine, Haley and Lord Jim Ferguson sipping scotch at the well-stocked bar facing the mantelpiece trophy case that ran across the beautifully wood panelled walls.

At this party there was a particular air of expectation. Haley and the Comets had just completed one of the most successful years in show business history, headlining the first major rock & roll tour, starring in two movies and continuing their string of phenomenal hits. Having conquered America the outfit was planning the first leg of an ambitious world tour that would introduce rock & roll to an international audience.

Little did Haley realize that this international market would be virtually his entire future. His U.S. career had peaked and by the time he returned from his foreign adventures Haley would already have lost his ability to make hit singles at home and his career would suddenly fall apart.

On Tuesday, 1st January 1957, Bill Haley and the Comets began the new year by embarking on the first leg of their world tour to Australia. At 11 a.m. Haley, the Comets and their

81

entourage took off from Philadelphia International Airport and flew to Chicago, where they connected with the Sante Fe Super Chief, finishing the trip to Los Angeles by rail.

Haley was extremely apprehensive about flying. 'Haley didn't like to fly,' says Ralph Jones, 'that's why we took the train from Chicago to California.' En route to California Haley made a brief entry in his diary: 'Crew in good spirits.' The observation, while optimistic enough, indicated Haley's sense of being removed from what was going on around him. This self-imposed detachment was the result of the habitual insecurity Haley suffered as a result of his blindness in one eye, but people would often mistake it for arrogance, especially because of his fame.

For the time, though, there was ample reason for good spirits. The Australian tour was the beginning of a series of fascinating, not to mention lucrative, trips. Virtually every date was already sold out.

On reaching Los Angeles they stopped overnight at the Ambassador Hotel and departed the next morning on flight 837. After a brief refuelling stop in Hawaii – just long enough for Bill and the band to acquire splashy Hawaiian shirts and beachcomber hats — the lengthy flight continued with refuelling stops at Canton Island and Fiji.

They disembarked in Sydney on 6th January and rested from their five day journey at the Gale Hotel, where Festival records gave them an elaborate reception/press party. Most of the following day was spent giving interviews.

The Australian public went wild for Haley, gobbling up newspapers with interviews and accounts of the tour. Seven thousand people packed the first two shows of the package tour, which also included Freddie Bell and the Bell Boys, Big Joe Turner, LaVern Baker and the Platters. All previous attendance records for Australia were broken and 10,000 people had to be turned away from the doors.

Haley continued to triumph in city after city on the vast continent. After weathering a rough flight to Brisbane the weary performers were heartened when they packed another 10,000 fans into Brisbane Stadium on two consecutive nights.

The *Brisbane Courier Mail* enthusiastically reported: 'Whole rows of the audience swayed in unison from side to side stamping and singing in time to the band.' The cheering crowds kept demanding an encore after the show, even after 'God Save the Queen' had been played to officially close the proceedings. Bill went back to the hotel and marked another entry in his diary: 'So far, so good.'

But on 11th January, while travelling to the scenic gulf city of Adelaide, Haley's luck ran out. The 1,100 mile trip proved gruelling and Bill's throat began to bother him. He was extremely tired and developed a fever, then he began to go hoarse. Despite the illness, the show went on and on the 11th and 12th Haley made four agonizing appearances, but the exuberant audience that packed the Tivoli theatre didn't complain about their idol's poor form.

The trek from Adelaide to the next stop, Melbourne, is a short one by Australian standards, only 650 miles. In Melbourne Haley was treated by throat specialist Dr Zelda Green, who had flown in from Sydney especially to care for the ailing star.

By the time the tour reached Sydney Bill was feeling better, and gave powerful performances before 86,000 people who'd come to the seven shows there. Both Sydney and Adelaide had banned rock & roll from radio play before Haley's concerts prompted the stations to scrap such censorship. Rock & roll was clearly what the people wanted, and the concerts had been peaceful events. Fears of violence and juvenile vandalism were quelled by the good behavior of the crowds, and rock & roll became accepted.

The tour returned to Melbourne to play four more sold-out shows. On 23rd January Haley and the Comets went to a preview of their new film, *Don't Knock the Rock,* then played two shows to 16,000 appreciative teens, while 8,000 other fans had to be turned away. A last triumphant return to Sydney, where audiences still couldn't get enough of Haley, saw the band perform seven more sold-out shows.

Despite such enthusiastic responses Haley remained isolated and self-conscious. The introverted star seemed to withdraw further into himself as the tour progressed. Al Rex remembers that all the acts shared a rooming house in Sydney. 'Haley used to lock himself in his room all day long,' says Rex, 'but Freddie Bell, this kid playing support, he had the charisma to be a great movie star. He would come out of the hotel room with his swim trunks on during the day and all the young girls were following him down the beach and he was signing autographs. Haley was up in his room drinking coffee.'

And making daily entries in his diary. The entries were all brief, usually just lists of the venues played, the attendance, and whether there were any records set. On a rare day off Haley jotted down: 'Visited aboriginal village. Met champion boomerang thrower.'

Haley and the Comets made Australian entertainment history during this three week stay when they played to more than 330,000 fans. When Haley left he was the biggest star the continent had ever had and his popularity has sustained itself in Australia up to the present.

The promotional mastermind behind Haley's initial Australian success was Lee Gordon, a one-time Chicago businessman who'd become Australia's biggest promoter. 'He went to Australia,' explained Ralph Jones, 'and realized the lack of entertainment there and decided to become a promoter. He promoted everybody. Sinatra was to follow us and he *refused* to follow us at that time because he was afraid that we'd done so well that no matter what he did it wouldn't look good.'

Al Rex adds 'This was the time Sinatra was down and out with Ava Gardner. He got to Hawaii and turned around and came back!'

The next stop on the band's schedule was a long-awaited English tour. The plan was to fly home to Philadelphia then after a brief stop-over take the *Queen Elizabeth* from New York to London. The reason for this elaborate journey was partially because of Haley's fear of flying and partially because of his desire to spend some time, however brief, home with his family before resuming the tour. You can sense Haley's relief in the entry for 27th January – 'Left for home', then again on the following day, 'Bad flight. Home at last. Thank God.'

When Lee Gordon heard about Sinatra's cancellation he desperately tried to get Haley to stay on, but the homesick rock & rollers refused. 'He offered Bill $100,000 under the table to stay one more week,' says Ralph Jones. 'He offered to fly him to England for the tour that was coming up. He said "I'll fly your wives and families over to England to meet you there." Bill turned him down.'

So ended the Australian tour. Haley had built a nearly

immortal name for himself in the country on a tour that must rank as one of the high points of his career. 'Australia was the best reaction we ever got,' says Ralph Jones. 'They loved us out there.' Al Rex concurs: 'I'll tell you, that's livin', man! Beautiful!'

But Haley was just glad to get home, where he only got a two-day rest. 'Slept all day and rested and played with the kids,' he wrote the first day back in his longest entry. 'Started to pack and get ready to leave for European tour. What a life.'

The next day, the 30th January, Haley's developing dread of the spotlight was reflected in the notation 'I hate to leave, nerves are real bad. Glad Cuppy is going with me.'

Twelve: The Second Battle of Waterloo

> I've been reading that my movie *Rock Around the Clock* has been causing a little commotion in your neck of the woods. Now I'm sorry about that commotion. I'm sorry about the disturbances and any trouble that followed. But I want to tell the kids who've been hollering for Bill Haley and the Comets that we'll be coming their way in February. And before we get there I think it might be a good idea if I kinda get straight with the rest of you good people.
>
> Bill Haley, from *Rock 'N' Roll Age*, a
> *Sunday Mirror* serial, October, 1956.

This and other articles promoting Haley were part of an extensive *Daily Mirror* media blitz to build up anticipation for his February 1957 British debut. The *Mirror* had, in fact, masterminded much of the planned tour which was instrumental in establishing Haley as a major figure in British rock & roll.

Even more effective, if less desirable, publicity was being generated by the rampaging Teddy Boys, the first postwar British teenage cult whose exploits with Edwardian suits and straight razors drove authorities wild. Britons were still reeling in the wake of the September '56 debut of *Rock Around the Clock*. The Teds adopted rock & roll as their music and Bill Haley and the Comets as the stylists they believed in. When the British press later asked Ted star Tommy Steele if he were imitating Elvis Presley Steele answered 'I was singing like this before Presley. Bill Haley's my man.'

The Teddy Boys slashed seats, sang along and danced in the aisles at showings of *Rock Around the Clock* all over England. A lot of other kids joined in the fun. Police in the Woolwich area of London broke up gangs of teenagers as they 'jived in the street' following a screening there. Six youths were subsequently arrested on 'Insulting behaviour' charges. Fifty rock and rollers brawled and lobbed light bulbs from a balcony at the premier of the movie in Manchester. Other cities such as Birmingham, Blackburn and Preston banned the movie altogether.

As far as the tabloids were concerned, the more controversy the better. A column ghostwritten by members of the *Mirror* staff but attributed to Haley titillated readers with statements like 'Bill Haley knows the facts about the kids who want to shock'.

Articles calculated to shock or arouse prurient curiosity offered Britons a chance to read about 'band chicks':

> She's a small town gal who feels she's got something extra on the ball, something too good for the local swains (hicks to her).
>
> This gal is no teenager (though she may have gotten out of her teens just recently) and she's subtler. She doesn't put on the rush act. If there are tables in the dance hall she'll occupy a small one as close to the bandstand as she can get. She'll sip her drink slowly, brushing off (impatiently, almost rudely) the local Lotharios who offer to dance with her. What she's doing is looking the musicians over carefully, deciding on her choice. When she's made her decision he knows it. Definitely.
>
> She'll stare at him until he is unmistakably aware she is interested. Then her glances let him know that she will not be offended if he steps over to her table during the next band break.
>
> And the conversation – with him doing the usual feinting and leading – makes it clear to him that an after hours date with this chick will not be uneventful. And it isn't.
>
> The next night the band is playing another town on its tour and the chick is happily contemplating the arrival of the next touring band.
>
> *The Daily Mirror*

The paradox of Bill's official wholesome image and rock & roll's sleazy reputation was explored in columns like *We Don't Make Boys Bad!* by Bill Haley himself. In the column, Haley defended rock & roll, consulting a psychiatric authority. 'The doctor said quite frankly that in his view some of Elvis Presley's routines carried a certain overtone of suggestiveness. If any of the adults in our generation look back at their own adolescence they would be able to pick out a style of music for expressing what couldn't be expressed through the channels that nature provided.

'And giving his views on that lusty number "Long Tall Sally" the doctor commented "I could pick out a few things like "We're going to have some fun tonight" but the words are relatively insignificant. I think if we take a poll of these youngsters and ask them what they mean by fun we'd find they really don't know." '

Haley went on to insist in the article that rock & roll filled the gap left by the demise of the swing era bands. 'Recording became almost exclusively singers, singers, singers and more singers – until rock & roll hit. The Comets are entertainers and we try our best to put on a show. But we try conscientiously never to act in any way that might be termed suggestive. And finally let me say this: I believe rock & roll artists can perform a special function in helping this lost generation find itself.

'We can show the youngsters,' Haley concluded, 'that fun can be clean.'

Accordingly, Haley laid down strict laws for the Comets against drinking on the job or picking up women on the road. 'When we were riding high,' Al Rex explains, 'he would not put up with alcohol on our breath, because we were playing for kids. He would not let us drink when we had a performance because he always contended the kids would go home and tell their parents "They were drunk." But we didn't need drugs or alcohol to go on stage. When they'd announce Bill Haley and the Comets the whole place would go up. If Bill found somebody with a bottle of beer in his hand he'd be fired the next day.'

Ralph Jones points out that Haley was particularly careful about sex. 'He was very strict. Don't dare fool around with any girls. None of the Comets. No way. And he was right. We always had these groupies hanging around and in fact all of us were married except Rudy and he said "No way, you want a chick I'll pay for one." He said "Look, we're the number one act in the world. All we'd have to do is get one of you guys in trouble with some young chick and there goes the act." He was right. He used to have a bed check once in a while just to make sure.'

Though kids were rioting at his movies and at his live shows, Haley kept insisting that he was being unfairly victimized by hostile elements. 'They say we're abusing the purity of the English language. They say we're creating hooliganism among young people. These charges levelled by the high brows and would-be high brows are just so much hogwash.'

It's hard to say whether Haley was just so out of touch with the kids he didn't realize how rock & roll affected them, or whether his statements were mere calculations, but he seemed to think he could prevent riots by just insisting that they hadn't, or wouldn't, happen. 'Rock 'n' roll,' he argued, 'has a respectable musical background linked with the very earliest American folk music. It shares a common ancestry with jazz – of which it is an extension. Rock 'n' roll is the great big melting pot of dozens of musical trends.'

The Haley life story was romantically embellished with folksy tidbits like this one: 'When I was sixteen, I figured I was ready to make my way in the world so I tucked my git box under my arm and hit the road headed west.'

Haley's American folk hero image was illustrated in this bizarre Americanese caricature from the *Daily Sketch:*

There once was a boy of seven called William Lincoln Haley who lisped 'Aw go on dad gimme a gittar .. gimme ...'

So Dad Haley settled for peace – he thought. From the moment William laid hand on the guitar peace fled. For William entered show business.

At 15 he was leading his own fevered jazz band at small town jamborees.

At 23 he was playing race music, the American label for deep south rhythm and blues.

With his kiss-curl and plump Liberace type face, Bill Haley has become the Powerhouse of the Big Beat. 'Thank Lawdie they go for my music and not for me' he says watching the personalised adulation that swamps kiss-boy Presley.

Haley is a dynamic worker. He beats fingers red 'n' raw as the Comets lash out the voodoo rhythm of 'Shake Rattle and Roll'.

Back home in Chester, though, it was a less than dynamic, in fact a shaken and exhausted Bill Haley who scrawled 'Home at last, thank God' in his personal diary after his 'bad flight' home from Australia. Again, the growing dread evidenced if his 'I hate to leave. Nerves are real bad' entry the day before leaving told more than a little about Haley's future.

None of this turmoil was evidenced in Bill Haley's column — as told to Noel Whitcomb — which was a regular feature in the

Mirror as Haley's British tour approached. The column detailed the day-by-day countdown as the band travelled across the ocean on the *Queen Elizabeth.*

'I haven't felt so excited,' said Haley in one column, 'since the night we found ourselves roaring along to a new beat – and christened it rock & roll. As you read this we will be boarding the *Queen Elizabeth* on our way to England, my mother's home. But tonight as I help Cuppy my wife do the last of the packing here at home in Chester as the children play happily around I keep wondering if I will wake up and find it's all a dream.

'Because it isn't long, you know, since we were playing for less than 100 pounds a week – and that doesn't go far when split up between seven of us in the band as well as a square meal for Jim Ferguson our manager.'

The ocean voyage across the stormy North Atlantic proved to be an unpleasant warm-up for a hectic tour. Bill, Cuppy, the Comets with their wives and kids, Jim Ferguson with his mother Charlotte ('She's seventy-seven but she wouldn't stop behind – no sir! Where there's "rock" there's Mrs Ferguson. She's a real gone gal!'), Jolly Joyce, band boy Vince 'Catfish' Broomall and others comprising the party of seventeen board the *Queen Elizabeth* on January 31st.

'Cuppy and I are just relaxing,' noted Bill in his diary.

The party had taken rooms in the cabin class of the boat, probably because there were so many people involved. But Bill would brag in his column 'I've actually heard people say "That Bill Haley has all the dough in the world apart from a few bucks owned by Crosby, so why is he saving a moldy few bucks by travelling cheap?"

'I want to tell you   prefer travelling with people who like my kind of music – the young people. And although there's absolutely nothing wrong with people who travel first class they are mostly older ones – younger travellers can't usually afford it. So I'm going with my kind of folks – folks who don't knock the rock.'

Dark clouds gathered over Haley and his young friends on the third day of the voyage. Haley noted in his diary 'hit rough weather'. That rough weather turned into a hurricane. Almost everyone including Bill became violently seasick. Ralph Jones recalls that his wife Dot was the only person in the party who didn't get seasick. 'One morning we were the only two people in the dining room for breakfast,' he says with a laugh. If the plan had indeed been to enjoy a relaxing ocean cruise on the way over it was a dreadful miscalculation. February is hardly the most pleasant time of year to cross the Atlantic.

'We are off!' exclaimed Haley's next column in the *Mirror*. 'Yeah man, we are on our way – rockin' through the ocean and rollin' through the waves keeping our telescopes at the ready to dig that crazy train at Southampton.'

But in his diary a disgruntled Haley wrote 'Can't wait till we get off this blooming boat.'

While Bill rock & rolled across the Atlantic 'in what my steward calls a light breeze sir, very refreshing,' fans read tidbits about the Comets, about Catfish Broomall ('He looks just like Elvis Presley'), and how Lord Jim resembled a Damon Runyon character from *Guys and Dolls*. They pored over accounts of parties in Noel Whitcomb's stateroom attended by stars on board ship like Victor Mature and Brenda de Banzie.

The fans also learned the history of the band. They read how Johnny 'Lover' Grande and Bill 'Mr Personality' Williamson met Lord Jim and Bill. How Bill discovered rock & roll: 'It was an accident. I back slapped the strings of the bass and instead of coming out the usual RROOM-PAH, it came out RRROOMPAH.' Fans were also given inside tips about how Bill and the boys wrote 'Crazy Man, Crazy' by taking the kids' favorite expression 'Crazy' and combining it with their football cheer 'Go! Go! Go!'

Along with the hype came a grain of truth when Haley expressed how stunned he was by the success: 'Sometimes I think I must be "crazy man, crazy" myself when I work out what has happened since that moment.'

DIG THIS

The headline shouted. 'It's the latest *Mirror* plan! A free trip on the *Queen Elizabeth* with rock 'n' roll Haley!

'Quick,' urged the article, 'Grab a postcard . . . a pen . . . a two penny stamp. There's not a minute to lose!

YOU

'could travel with "King Haley and his men" on the most

"glamorous liner" afloat from Cherbourg, France, to Southampton.'

The *Mirror* would fly two lucky contestants from England to Cherbourg where they would board the ship and sail to Southampton with their idols. There they would board the *Daily Mirror* Rock 'n' Roll Special train to Waterloo station.

All you had to do to win was 'Tell us in not more than twenty-five words on a post card the SQUARE you would most like to introduce to Bill Haley and WHY.'

Readers were also reminded that there was still room left on the Rock 'n' Roll Special train. Return tickets were available at 15s for the trip from Waterloo to Southampton.

IT'S GOING TO BE A GREAT DAY!

ROLL UP YOU ROCK 'N' ROLLERS!

Those 'rock 'n' rollers' who fleshed out the *Mirror* promotion rose early on the morning of 6th February. About 400 of them boarded the Rock 'n' Roll Special at Waterloo station to head for their Southampton liaison with Bill Haley. On the way they read Haley's column for that day's *Mirror*.

'This is it!' wrote Haley. 'Here comes the moment you've been waiting for. As you read this we shall be on our last lap to Southampton. What a trip this has been. The Atlantic has certainly shown us a new brand of Rock 'n' Roll. We've been riding the boiling sea today − but it has been a voyage we will all remember. And I'm hoping our British tour will be the landmark we will always remember.'

The experience Haley was about to undergo would certainly be unforgettable.

As Haley and crew prepared to leave the ship, a sizeable crowd was gathering at the Southampton dock. Reports later fixed the crowd at three to five thousand people. Six fans were chosen to present Cuppy with flowers.

'We had assembled with our baggage by the ship's gangway ready to disembark,' Haley later remembered, 'when I got my first surprise. There was a mighty roar that I thought must be the ship's hooter. Then I suddenly realized it wasn't. They were shouting "Haley" from the shore. From that moment on it was unbelievable.'

The crowd waited anxiously for the Haley party to clear customs. Policemen linked arms at the gate of the ocean terminus to hold back the shoving fans. As Haley emerged waving and smiling from the customs shed about 200 shrieking fans broke through the cordon. Police attempted to hustle him to a waiting car. 'I thought we were never going to make the car – there were so many people on top of it.

'We certainly had to dig that car – it sure was buried! Then, we thought we'd seen everything – the real onslaught began.' A swarm of teenage girls pounded on the roof and windows of the car. Unnoticed, the rest of the Comets watched incredulously. 'What the hell,' one exclaimed. 'Where do we go from here?' another asked.

Once Haley's car was freed of its unwanted passengers it made its way toward Southampton's railway station, where another group of fans waited. As soon as that crowd glimpsed Haley they went wild. He later tried to reconstruct the scene. 'A vast concourse of people with banners, streamers, stickers, badges and balloons – they all whirled together in a fantastic kaleidoscope of color and noise as we started floating toward the train. And I do mean floating! My feet didn't touch the ground for fifty yards — I was just carried along on the tide of people.'

The seething crowd clawed the buttons from Haley's overcoat, snatched his gray suede gloves and an overnight bag he was carrying. 'But that didn't bother me. They made good souvenirs for some of my fans. What did worry me considerably is that I thought for a moment that I'd lost Cuppy. She's not used to this sort of thing and it can be pretty frightening for a girl.'

Cuppy had remained behind, sobbing and cowering in the car. She clutched a stuffed koala bear that Bill brought back from Australia for her. 'I'm terrified of crowds,' she whimpered. Three policemen escorted her down an unused track to join Bill on the train.

Haley's police escort found it impossible to go against the crowd. They lifted Bill up and carried him onto the caboose, knocking over excited fans in their path. 'Nowhere in the world have I seen a welcome like this,' he panted as he was ushered through the train to his special car.

Security was tight. Police blocked every entrance to the train against gate crashers, while fans raced madly up and down the platform looking for Haley's carriage. One fan who was observed by a reporter from the *Daily Sketch* to be 'almost purple with excitement' stopped suddenly, threw her banner on the platform and sang in a cracked voice 'I ain't nothin' but a hound dog'.

As the Rock 'n' Roll special pulled out of Southampton the fans caught a final glimpse of Haley as he waved goodbye from his Pullman.

While the train moved toward its destination Haley had time to reflect on his reception. He jotted in his diary 'Docked at Southampton 2 p.m. and all hell broke loose. 5000 people almost killed us!' During the train ride the band entertained reporters with an impromptu jam and walked through the train laughing and joking with the passengers and signing autographs. Frank Beecher remembers the Rock 'n' Roll Special fondly. "All along the train route there were people by the track in different towns we went through. People were standing by the track waving. They knew the train was coming by – it had all been advertised.'

It was just rush hour when the Rock 'n' Roll Special pulled into Waterloo station. It had been scheduled to arrive earlier but a minor derailment delayed the train just long enough to have its arrival coincide with the attempted departure of thousands of commuters. Secretaries, typists and bowler hatted suburbanites were unprepared for what they encountered at the station.

'Before Bill's arrival,' reported the *Daily Sketch*, 'the platform was like a scene from a crazy technicolor film with chanting cats in black jeans, yellow jeans, red jeans swaying to the rhythms of improvised rock & roll outfits.'

Fans confined behind police barriers roared in recognition when they spied Haley at the door to his car. Flash bulbs stabbed through the air as cameras went off left and right. Four kids managed to climb over the barrier opposite the train. 'Two of the intruders,' reported *The Times,* 'saucy young girls, screamed their delirious delight at being so near Mr. Haley. But in a 30 second flash he was gone and they looked like lost sheep among the photographers.'

Haley dashed down the ten yard path from the train to the waiting *Mirror* limousine. He was followed by the rest of his party in a caravan of cars traveling between two cordons of police.

As soon as the crowds realized what was happening they surrounded the cars. Al Rex recalls 'They had these Rolls Royces
waiting for us – I was scared as a son of a bitch because the kids
were jumping on the cars. . . .'

The hundreds-deep mob pressed against the limos. Police
attempted to push them away as fast as they came. One uni-
formed policewoman was injured when she was crushed against
a car. She had to be rushed to St. Thomas' Hospital. Women
fainted. A hysterical mother was seen holding her terrified baby
above the seething crowd. Commuters wielded umbrellas
against the onslaught of fans. Shoes, handbags, banners and
scarves flew through the air. So many articles of clothing were
lost in the scuffle the station was forced to set up a special Lost
Property Office.

The car behind Bill carried Cuppy, publicist Suzanne Wade,
tour arranger Leslie Grade and reporter Herbert Kertzmeyer.
When their car was engulfed by the crowds Cuppy covered her
face with her hands and wept.

The limousines nudged fans out of the way and slowly with
the help of the police cleared their way out, then sped across
Waterloo bridge to the Savoy hotel. The fans were left behind
and were quickly dispersed by police and irritated cabbies who
honked and shouted at anyone who interfered with the flow of
traffic.

It was the end of what would later be called 'the second battle
of Waterloo,' one of the largest receptions ever given a star in
Britain. Reporters compared it to the welcome given Johnny
Ray or Billy Graham. 'Instead of hymns there was a continual
rendering of rock 'n' roll songs and cries familiar to followers of
the cult such as "See You Later Alligator," "Giddy up a ding
dong" and "In a while crocodile". But not all were fans for
several in the station carried banners indicating their preference
for Liberace.'

The next day *The Times* reporter reflected 'It may remain in
some minds as an enlivening episode in the rather dull routine of
normal rush hour.'

The *Daily Mirror* proclaimed Haley's reaction to the reception with the headline: *The Welcome of My Life. Fantabulous –
that's the only word for it – Fantabulous.*

'I heard we were going to get a welcome,' Haley elaborated.

'And we have enjoyed some pretty crowded receptions in the past, but never in my life have I seen anything like the razzmatazz of a welcome we got at Southampton yesterday.'

Since the middle of January fans had been queuing up, sometimes all night outside a chain of movie theaters to buy tickets for Bill Haley concerts. At the Manchester Odeon tickets went on sale at 11 a.m. on Friday the 19th but the crowds had formed at the ticket window by midnight on Thursday.

According to *Melody Maker*, Leeds ticket searchers sat 'Huddled in groups singing rock 'n' roll numbers from four a.m. and as soon as they went on sale bought out most of the 5,000 tickets immediately'.

In Cardiff a quarter mile long line of teenagers was kept awake by tunes played by a local record dealer while they waited outside the Capitol Cinema. The theater in Bradford received 1,000 postal applications. Rock & roll fans lined up there at five in the morning to buy tickets.

A wholesome image – always Bill's paradoxical strategy – was what the Haley organization strove to re-emphasize in the time between the docking of the *Queen Elizabeth* and the scheduled concert on February 6, at the Dominion Theatre in London's Tottenham Court Road.

Haley, Ferguson and Jolly Joyce had decided to take a hard line against critics who accused them of instigating riots. At a rehearsal the day of the concert Ken Robertson, a reporter for the *Daily Sketch*, saw a manifestation of this policy. 'Three hours before the show opened Haley and Ferguson threatened to tear up their contracts and return to America immediately if there were any mob scenes. Ferguson said "We're having no trouble. Everything is going to be happy or we all pack up. We have already warned the managements here after what we saw at Waterloo Station on Tuesday that if there's anything more like that we finish."' Moreover they vigorously denied any responsibility for the behavior of audiences and fans. 'But we're not going to be mobbed with the possibility of being harmed'.

In a *Mirror* column Haley urged fans to 'take it easy', expressing his fear for the safety of members of his party. 'I appreciate your enthusiasm – and the boys and I can take care of ourselves – I'd be grateful if you take care when the women and children in our party are around. For instance Mrs. Ferguson — "Lord" Jim's mother and my No. 2 girl — is seventy-seven and it isn't funny for her if she gets caught up in a melee.'

The London *Times* reported on the first Haley and the Comets show in England: 'Three thousand cats, alligators and other fauna from the rock 'n' roll circus packed the Dominion Theatre at Tottenham Court.'

The *Observer* commented 'The front stalls all at a guinea were an odd mix-up of people. There were rows of Teddy boys and Teddy girls, usually segregated – the boys nearly all short with hairbrush hair, the girls in tight black skirts or tartan trousers with their thick thatches of hair overhanging their foreheads like lettuces making their small faces look oddly the same.'

The fans squirmed impatiently through a fifty minute opening set from the Vic Lewis orchestra. 'The Lewis band played with immense drive,' commented a *Melody Maker* reviewer. 'The sax section was particularly crisp and well rehearsed.' As the Lewis agreggation announced their last number the audience applauded their imminent departure and shouted 'We want Bill.'

At 7:27, the excited crowd heard the sound of an electric guitar from behind the stage curtain. The curtain opened to reveal the red tartan jacketed Comets as they launched into 'Razzle Dazzle'. The audience went wild as the music soared, and the band responded by hamming it up. Al Rex split his pants, commenting, 'There's an awful draught down there.' *Melody Maker* described Rex: 'He threw his bass around with the abandon of an apache ill-treating his dance partner, then rode it like a Derby winner.'

Rudy played his saxophone behind his back, then lifted it over his head. When Bill introduced him to play 'Rudy's Rock' he said 'I hope you'll buy the record, 'cause Rudy needs the money.' The *Observer* noted that 'Rudy turned out his pockets not very convincingly.' As he introduced Billy Williamson, Haley quipped 'Give him a nice round of applause before he sings – he never gets any afterwards'. Franny was introduced as a baritone vocalist before singing his comedy falsetto version of 'You Made Me Love You.' *Melody Maker* pointed out 'Here as elsewhere, din permitting, he (Beecher) revealed he really can play.'

Bill was described by *Melody Maker* as looking like a 'genial butcher' and by the *Observer* as 'smiling like a schoolboy, strumming at his guitar, pointing it dramatically toward the audience like a cheerful machine gunner. He had an innocent, greedy look, slipping his tongue round in his mouth and looking upwards with boyish eyes, like a fat boy eyeing a huge ice cream.'

While writers had a hard time dealing with the performance critically, they were impressed by the enthusiasm of the crowd and the raw energy of the entertainers.

'Movement is the mainstay of the Comets act. The only man who sits still is the drummer. The rest twitch and jerk like devil dancers.

'The energy collectively expended by the Comets would just about propel the *Queen Elizabeth* back to the States.' — *Melody Maker.*

'The Comets spend their energies prodigally; they hop and shuffle and skip while they play and signal the end of a piece while jumping in the air and raising one leg. Their sole mission – to enliven the party. Mr Haley himself sways exuberantly from side to side, a happy smile unfading from his chubby well-nourished face. He pounds his guitar without mercy, and sings ardently into the microphone, perspiring freely the while. But there is nothing sentimental or morbid about his songs, his pelvis wiggles not with care (as does that of his rival Mr Presley, the alligator whom Britain is to see later) but with the purest joie de vivre.' – *The Times.*

Many of the members of the audience were bothered by the volume. *The Manchester Guardian* reported: 'The one thing that Haley probably does better than his predecessors is the production of sheer noise. The volume that he manages to get out of guitars, drums and clavioline is sufficient to drown a tenor saxophone whose player is turned almost inside out with effort. No mean feat. Still, when you are playing against an audience as this band is rather than to it, it behooves you to call in electronic science on your side.'

Security was tight in the theater. A large number of plain clothes police were in attendance — the word had gone out. If there was jiving in the aisles, no concert. Teens confined to dancing in their seats were remarkably inventive. As the *Sunday Observer* reported, '. . . a pair by the exit jived, still in their seats, swaying lower and lower: the boy next to the aisle bent right back to the floor. A cinema official hurried up, bending down at the bent body to make sure it hadn't left the seat, and smiling in admiration.

'The Comets kept the songs coming. Hands clapped, feet stomped, girls squealed as the tension mounted. "Do you love me Bill?" shouted a voice from the circle. Bill smiled angelically like a man who wants to be loved. He had the look of injured innocence. ("Nobody likes rock 'n' roll except the people," he said to the *Daily Mirror*.)'

Then came the finale. Excited fans jumped from their seats only to be collared by security guards. No sooner had the last strains of 'Rock Around the Clock' faded away than the curtain slammed shut. It was all over. In 30 minutes the Comets had whipped the crowd up to a fever pitch with 13 tunes, then disappeared.

Boos replaced cheers when the disappointed crowd realized that they were not going to hear more. The *Sunday Observer* described the scene: the audience 'started clapping in rock 'n' roll rhythm and shouting "We want Bill." More people stood up. More tall men appeared looking more anxious. The shouting went on.

'But there was still one weapon left. Over the loudspeakers at full strength blared out "God Save the Queen." There was a brief, anxious battle between "God Save the Queen" and "We want Bill." The Queen won. Never had the monarchy seemed so impressive. The Teddy boys slouched out, defeated.'

The next day a reporter for *The Times* speculated: 'Perhaps Mr. Haley's repertory is too slender to last a whole evening . . .' but guessed '. . . it is likely that he and his band are exhausted after having rock and rolled for three quarters of an hour. Perhaps their ears are tired too.'

After the show a *Daily Sketch* reporter asked Haley 'Will you give the audiences a longer act if they demand it?'

. Haley answered 'We just can't. I gave a longer act in Australia and tore my throat to bits.'

Ralph Jones remembers that Haley never did encores. He recalls that opening night: '. . . these people are paying good money to come to see you. That was one of the things we got roasted about in England.'

Tickets ranged in price up to as much as a guinea, which was expensive for those days, and the excitement proved fleeting even for diehard fans. 'Our first show was a huge success,' says Jones, 'but our promoter, Lew Grade, got very unhappy because we didn't do an hour, we did about forty minutes and those people were mad as hell, they wanted more. So from then on we did do an hour in England.' Actually they had only done half an hour which was extended to forty-five minutes.

Jones is skeptical about Haley's excuse. 'He claimed it wa hard on him to do an hour of that heavy music. Christ, we use to sit on the bus and do it for ten hours going down the road. To me that was ridiculous.'

Fear of riots may have been at least partial motivation for Haley's hasty departures from the stage. 'If he felt like it,' Jones maintains, 'We'd do an hour and twenty minutes.'

In the dressing room after the show Jolly Joyce spoke of his thirty-seven years in the business and assured the *Daily Sketch* reporter: 'But this is the act Bill does in America. Yessir, this is the act that got him to the top.'

Outside of the theater after the show fans surged in the streets hoping for another glimpse of their idols, not wanting the night to end. When the stage door opened and Bill emerged flanked by security guards, fans began to crush forward against the police barricade. Girls fainted and had to be lifted over the heads of the crowd in order to avoid being trampled. Others were stepped on and crushed. Minor struggles broke out in the mob between fans and police.

Even after Bill and the Comets had sped away in the waiting car the fans kept up the crush until they were finally dispersed an hour later. This was no full scale riot, it was just a scuffle.

Critical reaction was varied. 'Supersplendiferous,' acclaimed the *Sketch,* 'and just plain colossal. That's Haley and the Comets. The supercharged voodoo rhythm of the emperor of rock 'n' roll crashed into Britain last night with jet-age impact.'

The *Mirror* raved 'The joint jumped! The floor vibrated. Bill Haley really rocked the place when he began his British tour last night at the Dominion Theatre.'

A less enthusiastic *Times* reporter wrote 'Of art there is little in the Comets' work, though it is well studied.'

In an article entitled 'Haley's Comets Dimmed' published by

the *Manchester Guardian,* a disapproving reporter wrote: 'It is probably the height of pedantry to deal with musical niceties, but the point may as well be made since Haley seems to have overlooked it: the fourth bar of a twelve-bar blues sequence (the main basis of rock 'n' roll) is a diminished seventh. Do a thing to death by all means but don't torture it first.'

The sociological implications of the first rock & roll concerts were not lost on these cultural observers. 'What is its appeal?' asked a *Daily Telegraph* critic. 'Two young members of the audience, aged fifteen and sixteen and both from Hemel Hempstead, Herts. put it this way: "It's simple and easy to understand. It's got a beat and you can jive to it and sing to it. If you don't like it you are definitely square".'

'Haley,' the story went on, 'whose figures for sales of his records have reached the respectable little total of 22 million says "I'm really no ogre." With that kiss-curl hanging limply over one eye how can we doubt him? In any event I enjoyed the fun of the Haley type of entertainment. Let no cat call me square.'

As for Haley himself, the reception prompted him to write in his diary 'This is the greatest welcome ever given an American.' His international success was sealed. Almost all the theaters had sold out in advance and the first concert had gone relatively smoothly.

Haley was a good choice to be rock & roll's advance man. 'Mr. Haley turns out to be a nice kid, just like us, who drinks milk and wants to make young people happy,' reported the *Observer.* 'Rock & roll is a recognized cure for frustrations, repressions and boredom. Prince Charles' dancing teacher gives lessons in rock & roll. Television politicians approve of it. It shows that Britain is still virile, and robust. Like Marilyn Monroe, rock & roll has become respectable.'

Haley's good-scout respectability – especially when compared to Presley's unabashed sensuality – was the key to his diplomatic success. Of course, once the fans decided respectability was not what they were looking for it became a serious drawback. For the moment, though, he was in the right place at the right time.

Haley played three more nights at the Dominion after his successsful debut. The relatively calm opening night had, in the opinion of the Haley organization, vindicated him of the charges of causing a disturbance. Haley boasted that the scuffles at Waterloo were 'a publicity stunt that got out of hand'. His diary entry for February 8th read 'Dominion Theatre. All the press are waiting for riots but there will be none.'

Riots there weren't. Mob scenes were more like it. At the Gaumont Theatre in Coventry he noted 'Mobs of people paraded in the streets. Mobs outside the hotel. Show sold out – terrific.'

Sold-out crowds in other cities kept Haley's concern with fan behavior aroused. After the show at the Nottingham Odeon Bill was relieved to note in the red pocket-sized notebook which served as his diary 'No riot. Crowds unruly but OK.' On the 18th the band opened in Glasgow. 'Three thousand people waiting at the train station,' his daily entry read. 'We were mobbed.' The two night engagement in Glasgow drew mixed reviews. 'Haley clicked with a tremendous sock!' reported *Variety,* but the *Glasgow Evening Times* described the concert as the 'meaningless blast and blare of Mr. Haley and his assistant torturers. I have seldom seen such a second rate affair. The general effect was one of complete boredom. Even the cats jiving industriously in their seats kept glancing around to see if other people were noticing them.'

There was a raucous send-off at Glasgow Central Station when about 100 fans slipped into the station via an underground entrance, but they were quickly dispersed by police and the band was off to Liverpool. In Liverpool Haley intended to meet an English relative. The meeting was well publicized, but Haley's noncommittal diary entry for February 20th reads 'Met mom's cousin today, Mrs. Annie Bannister.'

The tour continued to Cardiff, where Haley was bothered by the 'Unruly crowds outside the hotel'. On the 22nd the band was scheduled to play the Plymouth Odeon. Haley noted 'beautiful scenery' on the way, then fretted 'Cuppy went back to London today to wait for me – I miss her.' After a stopover in Southamptom Haley returned to his wife, and his deep attachment to her was evident in the entry 'Good to be back in London ·vith Cuppy. Almost seems like home'.

Advance reaction to the tour had been so strong that shortly before Haley arrived in England an additional twelve dates were added to the schedule. This last leg may have been overkill, for on February 24th the London show was not sold out. The matinee at Kilburn's spectacular Gaumont State Theatre was the 'first show that wasn't packed' according to Haley's private notes. The next day only one of the two shows at the same theater was a sell out. Though the next shows were more successful ('Played to 27,000 people in three days,' Bill wrote) it wasn't enough to offset the growing fatigue and crowd nerves that plagued Haley. 'Really tired now,' he wrote in his diary. 'Wish it was over.'

Haley was obviously not happy about the additional shows, and by the time the tour hit Ireland he was really getting spooked. In Dublin rowdy fans congregated in front of the Royal Theatre, and after that night's show Haley noted 'They scare me'. After playing four shows in two days to 13,500 people a relieved Haley scribbled the entry, 'Mobs in the street but all seemed well'.

At the Belfast Hippodrome Haley and the Comets suffered the biggest disappointment of the tour. Rock & roll and the *Don't Knock the Rock* film had been banned in Belfast and Haley played to a half-filled theater. 'Damn it,' Bill wrote in his disappointment.

'It wasn't that the kids didn't like us,' says Ralph Jones, 'or didn't want to come. The church was very much against us, and the kids didn't have the money. Outside of the theater there must have been 10,000 kids screaming for Bill and they created a bit of a riot that night. This monsignor did come to our show and after he saw it he said "I see nothing wrong with it. I don't see what all the hullabaloo was about." But it was too late then.'

The Comets staggered through the last week of the exhausting tour, but when they prepared to return home after the last show they knew they had accomplished something extraordinary. For Haley, the English tour proved to be an experience he'd never forget. The same could be said for England.

Thirteen: The Well Runs Dry

WHEN HALEY AND the Comets returned to the States in March 1957, they were in desperate need of new material. They hadn't had a hit single in the States for a while and they had to put together enough songs for another LP. They were being eclipsed by other rock & roll acts and needed another blockbuster to stay at the top.

With this fact in mind, the results of four sessions at Pythian Temple recorded during a two week period between the 22nd of March and the 3rd of April are pretty incredible. For some reason, Haley and the Comets abandoned the hard driving sound that had powered them to the top for slick, empty adaptations of standards and trite novelty tunes.

'They were struggling with the music,' Frank Beecher recalls. 'They were struggling for good material. They were trying to come up with hit records and they were trying to do it on their own, trying to write songs themselves. None of them were professional songwriters, so they started to run out of ideas. What they should have done, what I felt back then was to hire professional writers and have someone write some hit material that you could record. Some of the stuff that they came up with was actually ridiculous. I don't mean to put anybody down, I think Billy wrote one, "(You Hit the Wrong Note) Billy Goat," and there was another song, "Paper Boy USA". I don't know, just ridiculous things. It could have been any title. It wasn't thought out, it was just thrown together.'

The session that produced 'Billy Goat' (March 22, 1957) included a deadly slow, pathetically unexpressive ballad called 'Miss You'. Haley's voice and interpretation sound so terrible it's almost unbelievable. 'Billy Goat' had some nice production effects but Haley's reading was poor and the novelty idea for the tune was thin, as was the other song on the session, 'Rockin' Rollin' Rover', which was about a 'cute' dog, perhaps a response to the huge hit Presley had with 'Hound Dog'.

The idea, it seems, was to record material inoffensive enough to pass by the conservative critics of rock & roll. Three days later they went back in to record more Tin Pan Alley style material. 'Please Don't Talk About Me When I'm Gone' is another plodding number, with Haley again using a stiff interpretation, hammering each syllable on the beat, never singing through the words. Pompilli delivers a good solo, but the tempo is so dull even Beecher is uninspired.

'You Can't Stop Me From Dreaming' presents Bill Haley as one of the greasy combed Philly crooners from the late '50s. The arrangement is good and the band plays well, but Haley's singing helps you understand why he always mentioned Pat Boone in the same breath as Elvis Presley when he talked about others passing him by. At least Haley could have done 'I'm Gonna Sit Right Down and Write Myself a Letter' at weddings and country clubs for the rest of his life.

Then there was son of 'Rockin' Through the Rye,' 'Rock Lomond,' an unfortunate return to a bad idea made interesting only by the production technique of inserting a country-style acoustic guitar bridge.

Gabler was versatile. He could record a Louis Armstrong, a Sammy Davis Jr, a Bill Haley, all in the same style if necessary, so he tried Haley out in a variety of contexts. Maybe it wasn't such a bad idea. Haley sounds less strained singing 'Is It True What They Say About Dixie?' on March 29, 1957 than a lot of other material he recorded, although his version of 'Carolina in in the Morning', on the same day is painful. Even a beautiful arrangement on 'Ain't Misbehavin' ', though, can't save Haley's lifeless vocal. 'The Dipsy Doodle' features a good performance from the band sparked by a clever guitar figure in the intro. As if to make up for Haley's bad day, the one instrumental track, Beecher's impressive solo spot 'The Beak Speaks', is a classic of its genre.

Five days later they were back at Pythian Temple one more time for more Lawrence Welk auditions – 'Moon Over Miami', 'One Sweet Letter From You' and 'Apple Blossom Time'. If you're wondering what relation the latter tune has to rock & roll, record the guitar solo on its own and when you play it back you'll hear the nucleus of a great guitar instrumental. Likewise, Beecher's intro is the best moment of 'Somebody Else Is Taking My Place', which also includes a nicely arranged guitar and saxophone break.

Gabler recalls driving down to Chester to help Haley and the Comets work out their material in the basement den of Melody Manor. 'I drove down there a couple of times, I killed a lot of time going down there though. I went down to try to get them to get things ready before they got to New York, and the songs weren't strong enough, some of them. You know they had the guys that were writing for his firm and I wanted to go down there to fix the material so that maybe when they came to New York I'd get in four to six sides.

' "Hot Dog Buddy Buddy", stuff like that I used to let him do. "Teenager's Mother", he would tell me like he's getting a reaction to it. It didn't make any difference to me because after it was done, I would pick out the releases and if I didn't like it, I could hold it up for six months, or never put it out at all. It didn't make any difference to me. To keep him happy, I let him do it.'

When the first '57 sessions failed to produce the kind of results Haley and Gabler had hoped for, Haley decided to revive the country and western material he'd been working on with the Saddlemen before they turned to rock & roll. Haley had never forgotten the days when he imitated Hank Williams and for the rest of his career when things went wrong he'd return to the idea of playing that kind of material. Gabler was against it, but on July 15, 1957, Haley and the Comets did what amounted to a country session.

One of the songs from that date was a good cover of the Hank Williams honky tonker 'Move It On Over', with some crackling guitar from Beecher in the intro. This is one of Haley's high points for this time. George Thorogood, who grew up not too far from the same area as Haley, got a lot of mileage out of this tune a quarter of a century later.

Haley also tried a remake of his first hit, 'Rock the Joint'. It's a nice arrangement, a good performance from Haley and the band, but it just can't catch the intensity of their earlier version. Beecher and Pompilli solos, on the other hand, make this take a worthwhile footnote.

Haley's singing on the ballad from this session, 'How Many', was unconvincing. His country voice, which had been sincere years before with the Saddlemen, had too much of the empty Vegas-style slickness in it by this time.

'He didn't have a voice for country music,' says Gabler. 'Haley used to get real set on some ideas. I didn't pick all his songs. I think I picked about 60 per cent of them. He had to prepare stuff before he came in, and he liked country music. He figured that country music could sell, especially in Europe, and he could get by with it there, but in America he never would have been able to do it.

'He didn't have the voice timbre for it,' Gabler explains. 'A lot of people think they can do country, they used to come up to Decca looking for country contracts but, boy, you have to be born down there and it's just in your voice, very few people can imitate it. Even chord-wise and harmonically, his mind didn't go that way.'

Despite Haley's lack of the kind of hits he'd become accustomed to in the U.S. in '57, he continued to enjoy phenominal success out of the country. A tour of Jamaica proved to be a spectacular triumph that may well have influenced fledgeling Jamaican reggae musicians. When the next album was being kicked around, Haley came up with the idea to do a collection of songs with themes taken from different countries and cultures throughout the world. This idea led to five sessions in November of 1957 which produced a total of fourteen songs.

The titles give you the general idea — 'Me Rock a Hula'. 'Rockin' Rita', 'Jamaica DJ', 'Piccadilly Rock', 'Pretty Alouette', 'Rockin' Matilda', 'Vive La Rock and Roll', 'El Rocko', 'Oriental Rock', and 'Wooden Shoe Rock'. For the most part these were simple tunes based on folk songs or melodies like 'London Bridge', 'Frère Jacques' and 'Waltzing Matilda'. The band apparently took the whole thing as an elaborate joke as some of their near-hysterical backing vocals indicate, but they play really well on a wide, if at times embarrassing, range of material. What's even stranger is how much Haley sounds at home singing obviously camp material – his voice is relaxed and natural on these tunes.

The rock around the world concept was a dismal failure – it's hard to imagine how they managed to get through 'Rockin

Rollin' Schnitzelbank' without totally cracking up. The problem was essentially that the material was lame. It was a low point in the attempt for the organization to generate its own material.

'Rusty Keefer wrote most of the lyrics for those songs,' points out Ralph Jones. 'They're all familiar songs to that country and what Rusty did was write rock lyrics to them. Rusty was a country and western friend of Bill's who was a songwriter.'

Another name that appeared on a lot of this material was Catherine Capra, Billy Williamson's wife. 'You know the situation there,' Jones explains. 'She belonged to ASCAP, so that's the way they spread the money around. She had nothing to do with actually writing the song.'

Gabler insists that Haley's refusal to use outside writers was a key in his demise. 'There were a lot of good writers, there were some black writers who I wanted to use for example, but he wanted to stick with his own crew down there in Philadelphia and they just didn't produce any good material.'

Song publishing is one of the most lucrative aspects of the music business, which is why Haley was so insistent on controlling the rights to material he recorded. 'I think it was money that caused the problem,' says Frank Beecher. 'When you write the song yourself then it's all yours, you become too hungry then you know, it's better to give it all away. If you get a hit record don't have anything to do with the tune. Don't even own it at all. It's better just to have the hit record. What's the difference who owns it? You go out and make money on personal appearances. Let somebody else write the song.'

The internal struggle for control of the publishing rights to Haley's material had already been going on for some time. It was a main reason for the rift that developed between Haley and James E. Myers, the co-writer of 'Rock Around the Clock'.

'My deal with Haley,' says Myers, 'on a handshake was he had to record one Myers music tune on every session. The first session we did "Rock Around the Clock", then "ABC Boogie", "Happy Baby", "Mambo Rock" and then we did "Rock a Beatin' Boogie". Five sessions over a period of a little over a year, it was no problem.

'So then they went in and cut a session with Gabler and didn't include a Myers music tune. I didn't care whether he wrote it or one of his band wrote it so long as I published it. When I came

108

back I had a little argument about it and he said "We'll take care of that". It was fine for another few months and then he went in and did another session without one of my tunes on it.'

The final rift between Haley and Myers came when Bill wouldn't cooperate on a television deal Myers wanted.

'Desilu Productions wanted to do half hour network TV shows.' says Myers. 'The format was to be *Rock Around the Clock* with Bill Haley and the Comets using a guest star each week and music. This was '57 – variety shows were big – Perry Como, Eddie Fisher, etc. They wanted to do thirty-nine half hours with a five year option. Haley was to get $10,000 per show and $10,000 for signing the contract. So that was $400,000 in front plus top billing plus 10 percent of world wide rights to the show. At this point the relations between Haley and myself were kind of strained.

'Haley was always a little insecure. Anyhow he always felt like someone was out to take him. Where he had that attitude from I don't know, because basically he was always treated, to my knowledge, fair and square with everybody.

'Jolly Joyce was sent into my office,' Myers goes on. 'He said here are the conditions that Haley wants to accept the Desilu deal. He didn't want to use songs by Frank Pignatore who wrote "Happy Baby" because he was mad at Frank Pignatore. He felt Frank wasn't in his corner because Frank was working with the Jodimars. He didn't want to use the Jodimars in the series. That had to be in the contract.

'I told the attorney in Los Angeles what he wanted, he laughed and told me to forget the deal. It had to be a multimillion dollar deal for Bill Haley he blew out the window and at that point I was really unhappy with Bill. I told him off good.'

Milt Gabler, who was at all the sessions and had a good idea what was going on, has his own explanation for Haley's split with Myers. 'Bill and Jim Ferguson and the guys in the band, they wanted to own everything they did themselves. They didn't want to share half of a song with Jim Myers or any other publisher. If I found them a song that they liked and they were going to record, they got on the phone immediately trying to make a deal with the publisher to get fifty per cent ownership of the song and saying they weren't going to record it if they didn't get half of the song. They did this when I already had the song

109

recorded, you know. It got to be a bad thing and after a while the publishers that had the good writers just stopped bringing material in for them.'

Obviously Haley's finances were in a perilous state of confusion. His decline was precipitous; because things were going so well in the band's trips to other countries the lack of U.S. success may not have seemed much of a problem at first, but the situation only got worse. Within five years of his greatest success, Haley would be a ruined man.

Fourteen: The Con Man's Con Man

In 1958 rock & roll took it on the chin. That was the year Buddy Holly died in a plane crash, Elvis Presley was drafted and Chuck Berry was jailed on morals charges. The stage was set for industry clones like Fabian and Frankie Avalon to take over the scene. Before long Senate antitrust hearings would bring the payola scandal to a head, punishing such visionaries as Alan Freed while rewarding the assembly-line types like Dick Clark.

It would have been the perfect time for Bill Haley and the Comets to regain their status at home, but the growing rot in the organization proved too much to overcome.

The year began on a promising note when Haley and the band went into the studio on the 6th and 7th of February to record an out-and-out rock & roll session, a welcome change from the bizarre formula recordings they'd made the previous year. 'Sway With Me' was a great r & b ballad led by Pompilli's full-throated saxophone playing and sung by the Comets. 'The Walking Beat' used a nice arrangement with some boogie woogie piano and a lively rhythm for an effect not unlike Danny and the Juniors' 'At the Hop'.

'Skinny Minnie' and 'Lean Jean' were the high points. Both were hard r & b tunes using a variation of the *shave-and-a-haircut, two-bits* rhythm popularized by Johnny Otis and familiar to rock & rollers as the Bo Diddley beat. Haley even switched his vocal style on these songs to the most openly blues-based singing he'd attempted since 'Rocket 88'. 'Lean Jean' was designed, obviously, as a followup to 'Skinny Minnie', both were excellent rock & roll songs which proved that Haley and the Comets could still do it.

In fact 'Skinny Minnie' became a fairly substantial hit – all Haley had to do to revive his sagging fortunes was record songs like that instead of the porridge he'd been turning out. 'I really love "Skinny Minnie",' says Gabler. 'The whole idea was mine, the basic gimmick – she's not skinny, she's tall that's all. Then we put some verses together in the studio.'

Gabler knew that Haley's organization was falling apart at the time. 'The band got progressively poorer,' he notes, 'because maybe they were travelling too much and maybe they didn't rehearse enough. They were away too much. When he came in he had too many things to do at one time. They didn't take the time to cook up the stuff and get it together. They weren't paying attention to business as far as I was concerned.

'By the time they got to the second year and it came tax time they had to pay the U.S. government their money. The money was spent. The manager didn't set aside their tax money on their earnings for engagements or for pictures or whatever they were doing. They were making a fortune, and spending it as fast as they got it. It wasn't an oversight. It was stupidity.'

Gabler recalls Haley's naive rise to stardom with a shake of his head. 'The first time I saw them they all had old cars. When I went to Chester, the cars were parked and the guys were all downstairs waiting for me. As soon as they sold five million records in one year they started to buy Cadillacs. They didn't save their money. We can't stop the money from going to Bill Haley. Columbia Records signs him to do some shots in films for $50,000 a crack or whatever he got, and he was getting $30,000 a week because he was a hit act. He bought a boat, his manager bought an art gallery. They spent the money and they didn't put it in the bank to pay the government. By the time the second year came along the government was after them.'

The Cadillacs did attract a lot of attention. 'He went out and bought *five* Cadillacs,' recalls Myers. 'Nobody can buy five new Eldorado Cadillacs, the IRS won't let you do it without paying taxes on it.'

Frank Beecher is still a bit in awe when he recalls 'He paid for those Cadillacs in *cash!* I don't see how that could have been good business.'

Haley's unabashed display of wealth did not sit well with a lot of people. Jim Feddis, a booking agent who'd handled some of Haley's early bookings and then was hired by Haley's organization to start their own booking agency, recalls that 'They were never in the black. Haley had a yacht and it was never paid for and they all ran around with Cadillacs. He was mad at me because I only had a Chrysler and he thought I should get a Cadillac. I said "I like Chryslers". That was his style of living. He bought an old house over on 5th street in Chester and converted it into offices. He had the top floor and his desk was on a raised platform so you had to look up at him like Hitler.'

Feddis, who was part of the Haley organization through what Ralph Jones refers to as 'the bad times', recalls that Haley's problems had been brewing for years. 'He probably had tax problems from the time he started. He had problems with Bell Telephone. He owed money to the dry cleaners. Fidelity Bank loaned them money, then all of the royalties went to Fidelity through Decca when they didn't pay. I first ran into them when they had a hit with "Crazy Man, Crazy". I was working with the Ingram booking office and I put him into Steel Pier and he sent us a check for commission from Ferguson and it bounced. Ingram and Ferguson had words, and Ingram told him what he could do with the band and I was working with Ingram so I couldn't book them. So then later on when I left Ingram they gave me an offer.'

As it turned out, Feddis went to work for Haley without realizing what would happen. 'I didn't realize how bad they were. I figured now that they are a big hit they must have money. But they never had money. They spent it faster than they made it. Haley was moody and dumb, and he thought he was smart. There is nothing worse than a dumb person who thinks he is smart. When Haley sat down and talked to you he was figuring out how he was going to screw you later on.'

Feddis remembers one moment when Haley's bad business sense caused him acute embarrassment. 'He was always behind in his payments to his first wife, and her father was in the police force. One day he came storming into the office and you could hear him a block away. He wanted to see Haley and Sam Sgrow, the office manager, is downstairs and he says "Haley is not in". He said "The hell he isn't in," so he marched up the stairs to the third floor where Haley had his office, pushed the door in, Haley was there. He got Haley to give him a check and said "Now if this isn't good I'll have you locked up." So Haley made sure that check was good. That was funny. It was a hot summer day and all the windows in the place were open. This guy really screamed.'

Unpaid bills weren't the only problems resulting from Haley's shoddy business procedures. Jolly Joyce, the booking agent who handled Haley's biggest tours, later sued Haley. 'He thought he was going to outsmart Joyce,' says Feddis. 'Joyce would have a tour lined up and then Haley said "Nah, it's going to be too hot then. Change that to September." Now Joyce went through a lot but I guarantee you Joyce was stealing from them too, besides his regular commission. But Haley used to laugh about what he'd do to Joyce. So Joyce ended up suing him.'

Haley's biggest problem, of course, was that he was surrounded with poor management. Lord Jim Ferguson was a small-timer from the same radio station Haley came out of, and though Ferguson's elaborate cons and hustles must have impressed Haley, the man was simply not sharp enough or experienced enough to be a top show business manager. Haley was apparently content to use Ferguson because he knew him long enough to consider him a trusted friend.

'Ferguson was strictly a con artist,' recalls Dave Shanzer from the Booth Corners Auction Mart, where Ferguson used to hang out after setting up his art gallery next door to the Mart. 'Everybody knew him. I got along with him pretty well because you can't con a con man and you can't bullshit a bullshitter. Lord Jim used to have two little chihuahuas with him and he couldn't wear a pair of shoes. He used to walk in here with his bare feet on the dirt floor.'

'Jim never worked a day in his life,' says Ralph Jones. 'He was a hustler in the true sense of the word. He was a generous man, though, he'd never harm you.'

'I never took to Jim Ferguson,' Milt Gabler admits. 'He was a big loud-mouthed guy and I always objected to the fact that while I was recording he's on the phone trying to make a deal with the publisher saying "I'll knock out the song".'

'That son of a bitch,' replies songwriter Bix Reichner when Ferguson's name is mentioned. 'He was unbelievably vulgar. He would walk into a room and push the girls aside with his big belly. I can remember him in Wildwood hawking for the group, saying "Come in and see Bill Haley".'

'Jim Ferguson was the manager in name only,' says Jim

Feddis. 'He was a stooge for Haley. Haley made all the decisions.'

'Jim Ferguson wasn't a professional manager,' explains Frank Beecher. 'He was just a guy who came along. In the beginning they were lucky, really. It was fortunate things happened the way they did. They couldn't handle it really. I think they became greedy. Different companies wanted to put out T-shirts with his name on it and wallets with his name on it, but Ferguson wanted a bigger percentage and the companies didn't put them out. Elvis Presley came out and you saw Elvis Presley wallets and T-shirts and neckties . . . they didn't get on the bandwagon.'

Ralph Jones corroborates Beecher's story. 'Jim made mistakes,' Jones says. 'When we had our office in Chester, when we weren't on the road we'd go down there in the daytime to rehearse, make records, do anything we wanted. But he liked to see us there. Bill would come in every day just like it was a job. Abe Saperstein called Bill up one day, this is when we were red hot, and he wanted to put out Bill Haley T-shirts, he wanted to do all the promotions on us that they do today as a standard practice. He could have made Bill and all of us billionaires. But Lord Jim says "We don't need that guy, Bill. We'll do it ourselves." Big mistake. Jim didn't have the capacity to do it. So he gets 1,000 ash trays made up, that's as far as it went. He *gave* them all away, he didn't sell any of them. Poor management, in that sense he destroyed Bill without knowing it.'

'That Ferguson, he was a joke,' insists Jim Feddis. 'I went up with him to New York at the Sheraton Hotel. He'd taken on a girl and we had publicity. So he stands up in the room, I don't remember what floor we were on, and just throws the leaflets out the window over New York City.'

'I think Ferguson destroyed him,' agrees Milt Gabler. 'It takes a strong manager to deny things to the stars. It's not just a question of ripping him off. I think Bill knew what Ferguson was doing and approved it and believed that what he was investing in was going to be good. But a manager to me is not just the guy who gets you the bus and the hotel reservations. He's also the guy who advises you financially and if you're in the fifty per cent tax bracket he banks it so he earns interest on it because you know darn well that on April 15th he's gonna have to pay taxes. Ferguson didn't have the know-how, and he didn't get the advice from the proper people.'

115

Ferguson's colossal arrogance was in evidence in his autobiographical newspaper account of the band's 1958 tour of South America. 'Here I am, the Old World Traveller, seated at Buenos Aires' world famed Jockey Club sidewalk café...' he wrote in 'Lord Jim's Letter', a supplement to the Wildwood *Independent Record*. 'I reached in my pocket, big-hearted like, to pull out a couple pesos, when Vince "The Catfish" Broomall, my eighteen-year old amigo, advised me not to carry my loot that-a-way, all mixed up with expense receipts, addresses, etc... I said "Look son, I've travelled the Seven Seas, romanced the Black Diamond Stewart, and I am widely recognized in thirty-seven capital cities and I've never lost a buck out of my pocket yet." But, all records are made to be broken, and mine was broken about three hours later, a pick-pocket lifted my entire roll, including three unpaid bar bills, in front of the Metropolitan Theater, same city...'

Ferguson was a reckless gambler who played cards for any stakes he was challenged to. His cavalier account of dumping the band's South American earnings through his careless, boasting attitude was not so amusing to the band members who found upon returning to the States that there was no money to pay them.

'We went through South America,' Al Rex recalls, 'to Rio de Janeiro, Buenos Aires, all over the place. When we came home, this is what burned me up, I went down to the office in Chester to get my salary and there was no goddamned money!'

Ferguson gambled big in business deals as well, and every one of them was a disaster. At one point he invested the Comets' money in a steel business. 'It wasn't a big steel mill,' says Rex, 'it was just a small fabricating shop. Five or seven people worked there – I think they were making urinals or something like that. The deal came through Lord Jim. These guys were friends of Lord Jim and they got him to buy in. I remember them coming on the jobs and talking to Lord Jim and Haley and the guys. They needed more money to keep the ball rolling. It went under and the partners lost x amount of dollars.'

Another liability from the tour of South America was the international booking agency idea Ferguson and Haley came up with. 'They came back with a piano player,' says Jim Feddis, 'that they thought was a genius. I heard him and Haley said

116

"You're going to book him, right?" I said "I can't book that guy. He stinks." The guy was smart enough. He had a year's contract and I don't think he worked more than two weeks out of the year.

'I can believe almost anything with Haley,' Feddis goes on. 'At one time I drove down to Ocean City and this guy from South America was really bleeding him. They were going to form this worldwide booking agency and management company. I sat there listening and thought "Are they kidding?"

'They were serious. So, coming home Haley says, "Well, what do you think of everything?" And I said "I don't think anything of it. It's a fantasy." They got so mad I thought I was going to end up walking home. He had these pipe dreams, but I don't think he used drugs.'

Poor returns from their business gambles weren't the only managerial errors Ferguson and Haley committed. Bill Haley, for all his faults, was a personally generous and good-hearted man when it came to his friends. He would surround himself with cronies and wherever his entourage went they lived well.

'Haley was stupid,' claims Al Rex. 'He used to pick up these goddamned bums and take them out on the road. Like [one guy I know]. He was with Frankie Lymon and the Teenagers. He got fired. Haley says "I'll give you a job." We were seven guys in the band and we would go out with an entourage of about eighteen or nineteen people, and most of these guys all they did was go get coffee for us.

'Haley would pick up a stray dog,' Rex continues, 'I don't know if it made his ego swell, he would pick up a stray dog and put him on the payroll. This one guy he met down at the shore, he was a Belgian kid that used to sing. He was a good singer but he was no rock man. And all of a sudden Haley just said "C'mon with us," and he gave him a job. Haley was that kind of guy. He felt there was no support unless he had a gang around. He could never do a show by himself.'

Of course crowds spooked Haley. Because of the blindness in one eye, he had no visual perspective, so mob scenes must have been incredibly disorienting. And, of course, he was extremely self-conscious about his blindness.

Frank Beecher thinks that Haley's self-consciousness was a big reason for his downfall. 'I think he couldn't handle his popularity. He wouldn't socialize enough with the right people. I've noticed over the years that people seem reluctant to give him credit for what he did. I can't believe how they could do the '50s without including Bill Haley when he had the biggest record in history. How could they leave someone that big unmentioned? There had to be a reason.

'He didn't pay enough attention to the right people. I think he thought he was bigger than he really was. He thought there was going to be no end, because I heard him make remarks like "We don't need 'em." But you *do* need them. He would be invited out to dinner and various things. Maybe we were invited to go fishing on a yacht, or to some executive's house for dinner. We would go and make some excuse why he didn't come. People resent that. I guess eventually that gets around.

'He was withdrawn, he just didn't want to be bothered. He didn't like to autograph, he'd run away from that all he could. He just didn't want to be bothered with the public. It wasn't that he didn't want them, it was that he was afraid of them. I always thought that he couldn't handle stardom. It was too much for him, he didn't know how to cope with it.'

Haley must have been deathly afraid of people asking him about his eye. It must have been a hard moment for him to get through the line 'I'm a one eyed cat . . .' in 'Shake, Rattle and Roll'.

Fifteen: The Germans

IN HIS NOTES from the tour of South America, Ferguson pointed out that 'Bill's had "crowd nerves" ever since his record-breaking tour of the British Isles', adding that the scenes outside of theaters where crowds tore his clothing to get close to him were making the whole organization nervous. If they thought things had been crazy on those tours, nothing would be able to prepare them for the European tour in October of 1958. There were full scale riots all through the tour, including what has to be considered the biggest riot in rock history.

On the opening night of the tour at the Olympia Theater in Paris, legions of fans pulverized chairs and streamed into the streets screaming 'Long live Haley! Down with the police!' After the dust cleared ten fans were injured and fifty arrested.

News of this event was well publicized through Europe, but it was just a warm-up for the swing through Germany. On 26th October 1958 Bill Haley played the first rock & roll concert in the tense, divided city of Berlin. The youthful inhabitants of this pre-wall city, victimized by conditions they had not created, were even more violently alienated than their French neighbors.

A lot of the kids on hand were East Berliners who were particularly resentful of the depressed living conditions in their sector. But kids from all sections of the city were raised in an atmosphere of violence and repression and they came to the West Berlin Sportspalast excited and angry. About half an hour before the start of the concert a crowd of whistling, shouting teens – all war babies – pushed and shoved their way into the Sportspalast and proceeded to arm themselves with improvised wooden clubs broken from the backs of their chairs.

At 8 p.m. the Kurt Edelhagen Orchestra began to play but the crowd, already restless, forced a premature ending when they rushed the stage. Hoping the appearance of the Comets would calm the crowd, the promoters decided to go on with the show. After clearing the stage of swarming teenagers, the organizers gave Haley the go ahead.

Soon after the band hit the stage they were in the middle of the most famous riot in rock & roll history. Beer cans rained through the air. Kids started smashing their seats, and each other, with their clubs. Whole rows of chairs were splintered. Many of the 7,000 people were whooping and howling, and a number of kids were shooting off guns loaded with blanks.

Ralph Jones says he thought the East German kids had deliberately planned the trouble, making it an incident in the Cold War. 'They were determined to cause a disruption. It was a planned thing. This was only, what, ten years after the war? Things were very tight politically. A bunch of these kids in their leather jackets – they all had sticks and motorcycle hats – started to march up the aisle.'

The Sportspalast director gave the signal for the eighty policemen waiting in the basement of the building to clear the house. 'We just got off the stage,' Jones recalls, 'before all hell broke loose.'

The kids went on to trash the arena, firing chairs at the cordons of police who formed a wedge around the stage. Spotlights shattered. Amplifiers were wrecked. Jones noticed that the police were reluctant to interfere. 'The political situation was such that the police dare not handle them. All they did was surround them and let them vent their spleen, just let them go. They took a new grand piano and turned it upside down. We got our instruments off, but the Armed Forces Network was there taping the whole show and they destroyed all their equipment.'

While rival factions in the audience brawled fiercely with both each other and the police phalanx, the cops brought in fire hoses to clear them out, but even after they left the arena the kids kept fighting.

The fighting outside the Sportspalast was referred to by the German press as the 'true battle'. Police used rubber truncheons and tear gas to disperse gangs of youths roaming the streets near the Dammtor Bonhoff. The crowds responded by smashing car windows and attempting to turn over a police emergency vehicle. It took more than two hours for the melée to break up.

The great Berlin rock riot was over. Damage was assessed at more than 30,000 Deutschmarks. There were seventeen injuries, eighteen arrests, one warrant of custody and twenty-two claims for damages. A former apprentice, seventeen-year-old Kurt P. from Charlottenburg, blinded a policeman's eye. A youth from the Soviet sector was charged with malicious damage of the speakers.

In response to critics who claimed the police should have been called in sooner, defensive officials pointed out that it was impossible to predict the reaction of the crowd to the police or, for that matter, the performers themselves. Director Kraeft felt it necessary to ban all further jazz concerts at the hall.

'Embarrassing,' was how Lord Mayor Willy Brandt described it. 'A disgraceful result of a youthful wish for activity.' He emphasized that 'A tumult of this type is not a typical phenomenon in Berlin but nonetheless a damage to its reputation.'

Youth groups blamed promoters, claiming they should be more 'conscientious with respect to youth. The model behavior of Berlin youth is well known. It should not be brought into disgrace by individual rowdies.'

East Germans seized upon the incident as great propaganda. The *Neues Deutschland,* the official East German Party paper, denounced Haley in a front page editorial for 'turning the youth of the land of Bach and Beethoven into raging beasts.'

During the German tour Haley and the Comets made a film with Arthur Brauner titled *Hier Bin Ich, Hier Bliebe Ich (Here I Am, Here I Stay)* co-starring Katerina Valente. The day after the Sportspalast riot the Comets went to the set. 'Katerina Valente comes walking in the studio,' recalls Jones, 'with a motorcycle jacket on and a hat and club. That really broke us up.'

The Haley tour continued to be hot action in the Cold War. The next appearance, at Hamburg's Ernst Merck Hall, produced similar results. *Der Abend,* a West German paper, reported that the concert began with relative calm. 'Scattered groups of teenagers stormed the podium and distorted their limbs in wild dances.'

This time the security force kept things under control as the concert got under way, but about halfway through the performance Haley apparently began to get nervous and fled the stage. A wild free-for-all resulted with kids once more splintering rows of seats and smashing whatever they could get their hands on before police routed them with tear gas. Damages ran to 20,000 marks.

Everything was falling apart, but for some reason the band decided to continue the tour. Ferguson kept claiming that a lack of police protection was causing the riots.

It wasn't really surprising, the way things had been going, that Haley's third performance, at the Grugahalle in Essen, ended before it really ever began. The audience of 6,000 was driven out at the first sign of any display of emotion by 580 police. Ralph Jones describes the scene:

'The German people hate the police, I guess as a result of the war, they *hated* the police. So the only way they could have the police, they put a huge curtain across the back of the arena and they kept the police in back of the curtain so they wouldn't be seen.

'So we start, and here comes some kids. They had potted plants all out in front of the stage and the kids started to throw them at us. So Bill stopped and we went off, the police came out and hustled them all outside. Now this was started by a few rowdies – the rest of the people didn't wanna leave. We got offstage OK and got up to the top of the auditorium where we could overlook the crowd.

'We couldn't leave, it was too dangerous to leave, they were all out there chanting in German "Bill Haley" or whatever. So this colonel of the police was there, he spoke English and he says "Watch this". Over the radio he says "Bring out the horses". So these mounted police come in with the horses and they're bucking the crowd trying to get them to disperse. Then he says "Bring in the hoses".–And they bring in these tanks with water that spurts around. Finally he says "Bring in the dogs". When they brought in the dogs with the long leashes, that dispersed them. It was like watching a battle.'

The next day the Ruhr town was celebrated in banner headlines that read: *New Brawl Around the Cowlick With Water Cannons in Essen.*

The impact of these disturbances was enough to convince the

governor of Barcelona, Spain, to cancel Haley's proposed shows there.

Haley's last German concert, in Stuttgart on the 29th of October, went off peacefully. The audience of 6,000 teenagers danced and stamped their feet to the rhythms, climbed on their seats and enjoyed themselves, but didn't resort to violence or spook Haley from the stage. 'When we were playing Stuttgart,' recalls Ralph Jones, 'Elvis Presley was in the service and he came to see us. He used to hang out backstage, he and Bill, and shoot the breeze. Hell, he loved us. He used to stand backstage while we were on he would be dancing there in his Army uniform all over the place.

The concert in Stuttgart was the first time during the tour that the band had been able to complete a set. After the show the audience spilled out of the Kellesberg hall and into a nearby park where they danced and partied into the night.

Despite this halcyon farewell East Germany claimed that Haley was promoting nuclear war. DDR Minister of Defense Willi Stoph pointed out that on the very day Haley arrived there had been an official decision by Bundeswehr Federal Minister of Defense Strauss to encourage jazz concerts in the country. According to Stoph, it was Haley's mission to engender fanatical, hysterical enthusiasm among German youth and 'lead them into a mass grave with rock & roll'. Stoph should have been a science fiction writer.

Of course, Haley was in a state of shock after these back-to-back nightmares. 'It was the worst thing I have even seen,' he said later. 'It was worse than anything in the States.'

Haley must have been hard pressed to understand what the hell was going on and how an ex-yodelling cowboy doing a Vegas-type live act could be causing all this commotion. In fact, he wasn't causing it: the music, and the era, took care of that. Rock & roll was destined to be a lot more significant than any of Haley's planners could have predicted. Despite Haley's insistence that his songs were only happy ditties kids could dance to, rock & roll had become the symbol of a generation. It was a vehicle for unprecedented emotional expression.

It was on the October 1958 European tour that Lord Jim Ferguson made his last big gamble as Bill Haley's manager. Lord Jim fancied himself as having a sharp eye for the value of a piece of art, and one of the businesses he'd set up with the money Haley made was the art gallery at Booth Corners. Ferguson had an unusual technique for acquiring the art works he promoted.

'I used to help him sell those paintings,' says Ralph Jones. 'I'd say "How much is this worth Jim?" He'd say "Whatever you think". We used to go down to the waterfront when we were in Europe, these artists were painting. Jim would buy all the canvasses, wrap them up in wax paper, put them in a tube and ship them home. That's how that worked. Then he'd put a price on them. He'd have the price on the back and he'd say "If a customer comes in, the value of the painting is in how much they like it".'

So on this particular trip Ferguson's acquisitional instincts got the better of him. 'We went to Milan, Italy. The train pulls in the station and Rudy's there, he says "You're not gonna believe this. Jim borrowed $50,000 from the hotel on Bill's name to buy some paintings. When Bill hears this he's gonna be fit to be tied. We haven't even played a job yet."

'When Bill heard about it he put Jim right on a plane and sent him home. But he paid the fifty grand.'

Sixteen: End of An Era

BILL HALEY AND the Comets went on recording without distinction or success. Their last significant hit, in 1958, was 'Joey's Song', a bright, tuneful, expertly played '50s instrumental that had a lot more to do with Italian folk music than rock & roll. The audience for rock & roll records apparently wasn't interested in what Haley was doing. For his part, Haley seemed to be aiming more and more for the older market, recording standards like 'Dinah', 'Ida, Sweet As Apple Cider', 'Marie', and a couple of other numbers that were collected. for an album whose organizing principle was that all the songs were about different women.

'They were good performers,' says Milt Gabler. 'They had their ride for a couple of years but it should have gone for much longer than it did, rather than just traveling around the world cashing in on their hits.'

Gabler tried his best to continue Haley's string of hits, but kept coming up empty. 'My thinking was to get hits,' says Gabler. 'He was still a Decca artist. But the figures were getting poorer, and there were guys like Presley knocking him for a loop. There was no question about Presley being the good looking guy and a great performer. He had a better voice than Bill, and he had good people around him.

'And don't forget, Bill never got rid of the spit curl. And he never took care of his audience properly. He just didn't stay the romantic figure. He can't blame himself for what he looked like but evidently he did.'

By this time Haley was so touchy about Presley that the other members of the group wouldn't bring the subject up. 'We never talked to him about it,' says Ralph Jones. 'See we were constantly trying to come up with something new. We tried to

125

switch around musically to keep up with the times. We decided instead of playing the same rhythm all the time we tried a few things with that eight-to-the-bar beat like in "Lean Jean", if you listen to it it's an entirely different rhythm from Bill's standard beat. We were trying to get with what was happening and it didn't happen for us.'

Al Rex, who would be the first member of this historic group to pack it in, played his final session as a Comet on 18th June 1958. 'When we were in England,' says Rex, 'I used to tell them "Look, this bubble is gonna burst if we don't change our style," because everything we were doing was the same. People used to say "Why should we buy this record? It sounds just like the last one you put out."

'So the one summer before I left, our sales were going down and we couldn't get enough bookings. I told Haley "Look, let's play for what we can get and wait for our record sales to go up." Haley didn't want to hear it. He had a boat down at the Wildwood Crest, down in Wildwood, and he takes his family down there for the summer and told Jolly Joyce, our agent, that he only wanted to do weekend work close by.

'We'd go to Wilkes Barre or somewhere like that and play maybe Friday or Saturday, but Haley kept saying he wasn't going to play anymore until the price went up. But the price wasn't going up and my contention was that we should have tried to get as much as we can until we get another hit record. But he kept saying "No, if they want us they're gonna have to pay." And that isn't the way the music business works.

'Jolly Joyce and him started having troubles and it might have been over the same thing, that he didn't want to work. Actually Jolly Joyce was one of the instigators of me quitting. He started telling me he would put me on top and get me a record contract. Actually I think he might have been using me to get back at Haley and I fell for it.'

At any rate Rex was gone and Rudy Pompilli's brother Al came in to play bass. On the 7th of January 1959 this revised combo went into Pythian Temple to record 'Dragon Rock', a feeble remake of 'ABC Boogie' with Williamson singing lead vocals, and a clever instrumental called 'The Catwalk' in which Beecher played guitar arpeggios to effect the sound of a cat purring.

126

Three weeks later they went back in for a desperation session. Haley must have known he was losing it judging from the lengths he went to change his vocal style on his cover of the Ray Charles hit 'I Got a Woman', in which he uses a very unconvincing southern drawl. He also cut the great ballad '(Now and Then) There's a Fool Such as I', a song that has proved to be a great favorite over the years. Haley did a very nice job on the vocal, putting a lot more feeling into it than usual.

Haley's extra effort failed to produce the desired results, and in what must be considered another desperation move Gabler brought them back in to cover the great r & b tune 'Caldonia', which had been one of Louis Jordan's best recordings. The flip side was a nice Ventures-style guitar instrumental called 'Shaky'. On the 19th June they cut 'Ooh! Look-A There Ain't She Pretty'. 'He could never catch the jazz guy that did that thing originally,' says Gabler, 'but he liked the tune. That was a big hit in his area when it came out and he thought he could revive it.'

Relations with Decca were strained by this time, and Haley's contract was up for renewal later in the year. Meanwhile Haley was setting up deals with other artists through his organization, and used the Comets to back up a local musician named Bill Fischer. 'We put out this record "Everybody Out of the Pool", says Ralph Jones. 'The Lifeguards was the name of the group. Bill Fischer from Reading, a good friend of Frank Beecher, played guitar. We put Bill out in the street after we recorded it with Bill and it damned near made it. That's what we were trying to do, promote other acts that would be part of our organization. We had our own label, Sunset, Jack Howard took care of all that. Joe Turner was down a few times and they were trying to promote Joe, put out more records of him and Joe was becoming part of our organization as an act.'

When Decca got wind that the Comets were recording under a different name and doing better than they were on the Decca sides they were making, it further strained the relationship. The real problem, of course, was that the Comets weren't producing. 'They weren't creative enough,' says Gabler. 'If you went to hear Bill Haley in a club you used to be so disappointed because the band wasn't set up so you could hear Bill Haley. The band would drown him out. That was all setting it up properly and picking up the instruments properly and the vocals. You couldn't hear his voice in the room, but you could feel the . . . rock group. You couldn't hear the words of the songs he was singing, but the kids all knew the big hits so it didn't make any difference to the crowd.

'When he appeared in the New York area I went with all the big shots from Decca, the executives, the sales department, they all went to hear. You couldn't hear Bill's voice. That's why I say I don't think he had enough knowledge about presenting the Comets.'

Even though things were tight between Haley and Decca, Milt Gabler insisted that it was Haley's decision to quit the label rather than Decca dropping him. 'I was disappointed when they didn't create,' says Gabler, 'and I couldn't create for them. Then I was disappointed because they became disheartened when the government attached the money that they owed for taxes and they had to leave the company.'

Haley and the Comets jumped to Warner Brothers Records, a new label that was looking to acquire some big names. 'Actually, when they attached his earnings,' Gabler points out, 'he still had to work out his contract and finish his contracts.' In November of 1959 the band went in with Gabler and finished their obligation with a handful of instrumentals, including covers of 'Music, Music, Music' and 'Mack the Knife'.

'Bill was in trouble for money,' continues Gabler, 'and his sales had dropped off. If you wanted a $50,000 a year guarantee at that point the sales wouldn't vindicate it. The government had already served us with papers on back taxes for Bill Haley. So if he got $25,000 a year instead of a $50,000 guarantee they would pick up $20,000 of it. He wouldn't see the money.

'So he said "I can get the money from Warner Brothers." The IRS didn't know he was going to Warner Brothers so they haven't attached his money there. And if he got it in advance Bill had money in his pocket.

'I was a friend. I said "Go to Warner Brothers." I told him the government should get the money, but here was this guy that came from the top of the hill and was sliding down to the bottom fast. I couldn't stop him or advise him legally or anything.

'I can't blame Bill's failure on Ferguson,' Gabler concludes. 'I have to blame it on Bill. Bill did not know enough about the ordinary rudiments of doing business. He knew what kind of

Haley and Jack Howard in their Chester office. Note the picture of Haley and Elvis Presley on the wall. *Rex Zario Collection*

Rudy Pompilli. *Rex Zario Collection*

Above: Bill Haley and the Comets. *Back, left to right:* Billy Williamson, Rudy Pompilli, Bill Haley, Ralph Jones, Frank Beecher. *Kneeling:* Al Rex, Johnny Grande. *Decca Records*
Below: Ralph Jones and Haley – the Old Romantics. *Rex Zario Collection*

Daily Mirror

WED FEB 6 1957

2ᵈ FORWARD WITH THE PEOPLE
No. 16,532

HOW THE MIRROR BROUGHT THE KING OF ROCK 'N' ROLL TO HEP-HEP-HAPPY LONDON

FANTABULOUS!

BILL HALEY'S OWN STORY of

The welcome of my life!

EXCLUSIVE .... PAGE 2

FANTABULOUS! That is the only word to describe the welcome to Bill Haley yesterday, seen here with blonde wife (front) and fans aboard the Mirror's Rock 'n' Roll choo-choo on the way to London.
More fantabulous pictures on CENTRE and BACK PAGE

The *Daily Mirror* celebrates Haley's arrival in England in 1957. *Syndication International Ltd*

★ ☆ ★ ☆ HEY, CATS—DIG THAT DOCKSIDE ROCK!!!

HERE'S Haley (picture right). And just look at those excited crowds on the dockside at Southampton yesterday.

They are seen welcoming the Rock 'n' Roll King after he arrived in the liner Queen Elizabeth. Police had to clear a path for Bill as he struggled to reach the Mirror's special Rock 'n' Roll Choo-choo which took him to London.

FANCY PANTS

☆ Dig those special jeans, worn by Sylvia ☆ Wakefield, 17 (left), and Diane Thomson, 15. They said they sat up all night embroidering Bill's name on them.

HERE'S HALEY!

Follow the arrow, Cats! Yep, at the end of it is the Rock 'n' Roll King himself, surrounded by Cats (and cops) at Southampton yesterday as he fought his way to the Mirror's special train. Man, WHAT a welcome!

ROCK 'N' ROLL STRIP

They call him RORY—Rory Blackwell, leader of a Rock Band which welcomed Bill Haley and his Comets when they arrived at Waterloo Station yesterday. And Rory really was roaring. Dig that crazy caper!

● Rock Around The Clock shirt—worn by hep-cat Marie Imlah, of Glasgow, at Waterloo.

● Champagne for Haley? No, sir. Bill gets rockin on MILK.

● A cop lies on Bill Haley's car roof at Waterloo. More cops sit on the bonnet. Not TOO near, please!

● Girls lost their shoes in the rush to see Bill. Here for the big sell-out after the Battle of Waterloo.

Left: Haley's triumphant return to Great Britain, April 1968. *Right:* British rocker Freddie 'Fingers' Lee presents Haley with a 78 rpm record of 'Rock Around the Clock' from his own collection in May 1968. Rudy Pompilli is on the right. *Syndication International Ltd*

Left: Haley demonstrates dance steps to swinging London in May '68. *Right*: Haley playing 'Rock Around the Clock' in London, March 1974.

Syndication International Ltd

Haley after a performance during his '74 UK tour. *Syndication International Ltd*

records he wanted to make and what sound he wanted to get but he didn't have enough musical knowledge to produce what he wanted. So he got with people that were exploiting him or non-musical people that couldn't put the records together. If he wasn't making "Rock Around the Clock" what else was he gonna do? And it's sad. He should have hired responsible people. Especially when he could afford it.

'Poor man. To have it all in his hands like that and just let it go.'

Haley made a two year deal with Warner Brothers. For the first record on the new label, he quite naturally returned to the style he was most familiar with, country and western. The somewhat inappropriately titled *Bill Haley's Juke Box* failed to capture the imagination of the public and Haley ended up promoting the record back on the local radio station in Chester by playing one song a week from the LP over the air.

The follow-up record was also a failure and Haley's Warner Brothers era ended abruptly. 'Warner Brothers couldn't get the Decca sound,' Ralph Jones notes. 'We went to Warner Brothers hoping to get a new shot in life but it proved to be nothing. They just didn't buy our records. Of course, the tunes we recorded for Warner Brothers were terrible. I never liked any of them really even though we re-recorded "Rock Around the Clock". The first thing they put out on us was "Candy Kisses" and "Tamiami". It was a fiasco.'

There was a growing sense among the Comets that they'd reached the end of the trail. 'The whole thing went to pot later,' says Jones. 'You know how I could tell it was over? We were playing in Toronto, Canada. They always had police to lead Bill up to the stage and off the stage. Well they led him off the stage this one night, we had a good crowd, nice show, Rudy and I were walking behind him. There wasn't a goddamned soul come up and ask him for an autograph or even try to get near him and I said "Rudy, it's over".'

Jones became the second of the classic Comets to leave the fold. 'Not bragging, but I was the smartest one of the bunch,' he says with a laugh. 'Well, Rex was a little smarter, he got out a little before I did. I was lucky, I stepped in when everything big happened and got out before the bottom fell out. It wasn't too good when I left. Haley was still living in that little dream world.

One thing about this business, you have to learn when to get out, and that's something he never really learned.

'As soon as someone new comes along the kids take to it. It's a fickle business. When Presley came in strong he really knocked us out of the box. Lucky for Bill he cut "Rock Around the Clock" because this is a crazy business – it's all luck and fate and being there at the right time. If they'd never have made *Blackboard Jungle* you'd probably never have heard of Bill Haley's Comets.

'Even though we made good money we spent it. Lord Jim would buy $100,000 worth of paintings on Bill's name, and then Uncle Sam comes in there. Believe me, none of this was Bill's fault. He envisioned all of us becoming millionaires. I'm sure that he's totally innocent of all that because he trusted people to do their jobs and these guys didn't do 'em. Ferguson wasn't totally responsible but he helped.'

Seventeen: The Twist King

HALEY WENT UNDERGROUND after the Warner Brothers fiasco, recording for whatever small label came along. Oddly enough, he scored a dramatic success almost immediately in Mexico, where an instrumental with chanted vocals from the Comets and virtually no performance by Haley himself called 'Florida Twist' became the biggest selling single in Mexico's history. 'Florida Twist' had little to do with the twist – it sounded more like a Boots Randolph number, with Rudy Pompilli's saxophone dominating the arrangement – but it was sung in Spanish and had a big name associated with it, so once again Haley was able to trade in on a kind of cultural exchange program to bolster his sagging career.

'Florida Twist' was actually a musical rejuvenation for the Comets after the horrible recordings that finished out the Decca contract and died on the vine with Warner Brothers. The instrumental concept enabled the Comets to rely on their playing and arrangement skills, which were still considerable. Other instrumentals recorded in Mexico flashed the Comets' genius. 'Pure De Papas' ('Mashed Potatoes') is reminiscent of 'Tequila', with excellent Pompilli and Beecher soloing, Grande playing some Professor Longhair style New Orleans piano and an unidentified vocalist shouting occasional interjections in Spanish. 'Comet Boogie', 'Nocturno De Harlem', 'Silbando y Caminando', 'Tren Nocturno' and 'El Madison' are all fine instrumental performances, ranging from big-band swing to r & b, which ride on Pompilli and Beecher solos.

Unfortunately, the quality of these rare Mexican Haley recordings for Orfeon Records is uneven at best. 'El Blues De Los Cometas' rides a nice Beecher guitar figure for a while but is so poorly recorded that the guitar line fades in and out of the mix.

131

On 'Negra Consentida', 'Mish Mashed' and 'Mas Twist' ('Let's Twist Again') Haley sings in Spanish, not very convincingly, though he does bring a lot of emotion to the ballad 'Cerca Del Mar'.

Haley and the Comets did a number of cover versions of other hits like 'Puerta Verde' ('Green Door'), 'No Te Puedes Sentar' ('You Can't Sit Down'), 'Baja California Sun', a slight rewrite of 'California Sun', and 'Nueva Orleans' ('New Orleans'). At the beginning of the 'live' version of 'Land of 1000 Dances' you can hear Joe Turner's introduction: 'Now ladies and gentlemen here's Mister Go Go − Beel Haley − and his Comets. Let 'em roll'. Turner's career had been revived by Haley in Mexico and the two singers became close friends.

The saddest moments of Haley's Mexican recording career were the pathetic remakes of his Decca hits − 'Rock Around the Clock', 'Rip It Up', 'Razzle Dazzle', 'La Marcha De Los Santos' ('When the Saints Go Marching In'), 'Hay Nos Vemos Cocodrilo' ('See You Later Alligator') and 'Boogie ABC'.

Haley's lack of musical achievements in Mexico was offset by his continued status as a superstar there. 'I liked Mexico,' says Frank Beecher. 'It was an awfully fascinating scene. I had a good time doing the Mexican records. It was a great adventure, really. It was a lot of fun. I'd never been away from home before except being in the army. I never travelled to that extent, I was with Benny Goodman but it wasn't as glorious. Benny Goodman was the star, but in Haley's group each fellow in the band was looked up to. They didn't just go up to Bill Haley, they came to all of us as individuals.'

The last tour Ralph Jones made with the Comets was in April 1960 when they played throughout Mexico. During that time they made several films. 'All they were was a nightclub scene really. We weren't even in the feature − I've never seen the films and to this day I don't know what the plots were. We were basically just shown in nightclub scenes. Of course they used the name to draw people in.'

Jones recalls Mexico as an opulent place. 'They had beautiful nightclubs there. The clubs down there are unbelievable. We went to a club as guests and the show was the *Scheherazade* suite. They had a fifty piece orchestra, chorus girls coming down from all over the place, I never saw anything like it.'

It was during one of these Mexican tours that Haley became attracted to a dancer who was performing with the group. Martha Velascao would later become Haley's third wife, but when Haley first took up with her it shocked the members of his band.

'At that point he was beginning to get involved with her,' says Frank Beecher, 'which surprised all of us. He was a devoted family man and he always laid it on the line to the guys in the band – if we got caught fooling around we'd be fired. He didn't tolerate anything like that.'

That wasn't the only cardinal rule of Comet behavior broken by Haley in Mexico. The extensive alcohol abuse that would later contribute to his disintegration began in earnest about this time. 'He always drank,' Beecher says, 'but it became heavier and heavier, you know. People who become successful find a way to destroy themselves.'

Back in the States, the situation worsened, and upon returning from a tour of Mexico the Comets revolted. On record the band had deteriorated into a twist act, as an album recorded live in 1961 for Roulette Records called *Twistin' Knights At the Round Table* documents. The band played before a noticeably bored crowd, running through 'Florida Twist', 'Twist Marie', 'Queen of the Twisters', 'Caravan Twist' and a twist *waltz*, 'One-Two-Three Twist'. The record does include a few fine instrumental moments – 'Lullaby of Birdland Twist', 'Whistling and Walking Twist' and the astonishing 'Down By the Riverside Twist' which features one of Beecher's finest moments as a guitar soloist. *Nobody* played guitar like that back then.

Financial troubles finally broke up the Comets. 'There were a lot of payments I never received,' says Beecher. 'I never got anything from the Mexican recordings at all, and I wrote a couple of those things. In Mexico we had some problem retrieving money. People who handled the money, promoters, instead of paying you when the job was over they'd disappear. It costs a lot of money to keep a group on the road like that because, you know, we stayed first class.'

Disillusioned with the direction things were taking, Beecher finally quit, and shortly after him, the others left as well. 'It was a big let-down,' says Beecher. 'That's why I came home. I went to work in a factory, in fact I'm still working for the same company. I decided I was just going to play music on the weekends and work for a living. You put so much into it and then everything caves in around you. It's a bad feeling when there's nowhere to go but down.'

Even though all the Comets left about the same time in 1962, Beecher insists that it was 'not a conspiracy. When I left I left on my own. I just told Bill I couldn't go on. Things were deteriorating. My paycheck wasn't coming up every week. I said "This is a business, not a game". I saw the thing deteriorating and I didn't want to go down with it.'

John Grande, who followed Beecher out, says 'None of us really came out of it with anything. Some of the band members got tired of being on the road all the time. Some of the fellows did want to settle back down. The way we were on the road like we were I don't think anybody's marriage was getting any better. Mine didn't.'

Haley's marriage with Cuppy hit the rocks. A broken man who'd lost his money, his band and his wife, Haley's final blow came when he even lost his cherished house, Melody Manor. 'He lost all his property', Al Rex recalls. 'They sheriffed him out. I remember Franny Beecher telling me they went to Mexico and they didn't have any money to pay the band.'

Haley fled to Mexico in disgrace, leaving behind a sorrowful trail of enemies and unpaid bills. He moved to Mexico, married Martha Velascao and started yet another family. 'He might have gone down to Mexico', theorizes Milt Gabler, 'because there he could do a gig and pick up the whole check without paying tax at the box office.'

Gabler was one of many people Haley left owing money. 'I never got a statement or a nickel from Bill Haley's publishing company on any record I ever made,' says Gabler. 'Jack Howard came to me in my New York office and wanted to buy "Skinny Minnie" from me because it was a hit in Europe and I'd get some money if I'd release the copyright to them. I said "I'll do it in a minute". I never got any money from Bill's firm anyway. I said "But you gotta pay me the money you owe me on this song." He brought me a check for thirty-eight dollars and change. I signed the release and he gave me my check. I deposit the check and it was rubber! It bounced. I didn't even call Howard. I said "That keeps the Bill Haley record with me absolutely straight!" Now I can say I never got a penny from him on any of his songs. I never even called Jack. I never saw him again. I have the check somewhere. I kept it. If it was $380.00 maybe I would have chased him on it, but $38.00, I looked at it skeptically when he gave it to me. I'm glad it bounced.'

One of the most touching aspects of the Haley story is that Rudy Pompilli decided to go back with him after leaving with the rest of the Comets. Pompilli had been playing with Ralph Jones in a local group back in Chester when he made the decision to rejoin Haley.

'Rudy came to me one night', Jones recalls, 'we were doing very well, making a buck. We weren't making a lot of money but he was home. He didn't like traveling, he wasn't hassled, and it was a good group musically, he could play more of what he likes to play. He came up to me and said "Ralph, I'm going back". I said "Man, haven't you had enough"? He says "Bill called me and I just feel I outta go back".'

Pompilli would stay with Haley through all the nightmare years that followed, putting together his bands, nursing him through his psychotic episodes, even sometimes paying his bills. Most of all, Pompilli remained Haley's staunch and loyal friend to the day he died.

Eighteen: Rock & Roll Revival

IN 1964 MILT Gabler got a phone call from Bill Haley. It was the first time he'd heard from his former associate in five years. 'He called me on the phone,' says Gabler, 'and he said "Milt, you were the greatest thing that happened to me in my whole life. You always played it straight with me. I think you could make hits with us once again and get the sound back that we used to have." So I said "Well, Bill, I'll try." I went up and saw the vice-president in charge of sales and I said "Look, maybe Haley can do it again and the poor guy is down and out." We had made a lot of money for him and ourselves in the old days. So we gave him another shot.

'So I asked Bill what he wanted to do. "I've got two songs," he says. "I think I can bring back Jim Lowe's 'Green Door' and then I have a piece of material called 'Yes, She's Evil'." So we did these two sides, but they didn't happen. "Green Door" has a good sound, though.'

Gabler is still disappointed that he couldn't revive Haley's career. 'I would have loved to have had the glory,' he says. 'I used to give a lot of singers a chance that had been stars earlier. "Bring them back alive Gabler" they called me, like Frank Buck. Because I always feel when an artist had it at one time if they don't lose their vocal chords physically, if they've got the energy and the muscles in the throat, if you get the right arrangement and the right piece of material the odds are you can have a hit again. But the trouble is the company only let me make two sides with him. They would just give you the shot for old times sake. And we didn't hit a home run so Bill only stayed for two sides.'

At this point Haley had indeed flopped in his homeland – live performances even included a section where he would don a

Beatle wig. But Haley still had a legitimate claim to the rock crown outside of the U.S. He wasn't just the biggest selling rock & roll artist in Mexico — his following in Europe and Australia was still formidable. He played to 30,000 people in Berlin during June of 1964 and made a spectacular return to England.

Haley had been paired with the Manfred Mann group on this tour, but his old fans came out in force to root for him and heckled Mann on the first gigs when he followed Haley's set. He had quickly re-established his headlining potential in England.

British press dubbed Haley 'the father of rock & roll' on this tour, and he began to elaborate on his previous role as a spokesman for the music. 'The way I see it,' he said, 'is that I carried it for a while and now it's carrying me. But what happened with me is what happens to almost every other performer. The public got saturated. Every day there was something about Bill Haley. And all the time people were coming to me and asking "Bill, when is rock & roll going to die?" And I'd say "It's never gonna die." Now I get asked "How long is it gonna last?" That's the difference.'

The idea of a rock & roll revival was already in the formative stages for Haley. 'It seems like we are virtually in the class with Louis Armstrong or a Glenn Miller,' he said, 'known as veterans of our trade, originators of a style of music. A good many of our bookings come from many parts of the world where people want to be nostalgic about rock & roll. We have always been defenders of rock and now we find ourselves showing how it is played, describing it to people and generally keeping it alive. We prefer to play the places where we feel the music is dying and needs someone to stir up the interest once again.'

During the late '60s and early '70s, Haley spearheaded a revival of interest in '50s rock & roll. In '66 he played a triumphant tour of Europe which included a legendary concert in Paris at the Alhambra Theater where he blew a bill of '60s rock bands off the stage. Haley's account of his success with the rock & roll revivals is poignant.

'I had been doing the Army bases in Europe,' he told Ken Terry in his final interview, 'and I was really down. I thought "What am I doing? I'm getting older, these young kids are coming along. Maybe I'm on the wrong kick." I was feeling sorry for myself. I had a guy who flew over from England named Patrick Malynn who today is still my European manager. He flew over and said "Bill, I got an offer for you to play the Alhambra Theater in Paris. We're going to do a rock show there, and they want you on the bill with current English rock acts."

'Since I was already in Frankfurt, Germany, I said "All right, we'll play it on the way back." And we went in really down, man, I mean, I remember coming out of the dressing room and one of the girl friends of one of the musicians – I forget which act it was – as I came out said "Are you still alive?" Man, you talk about cutting you down. And I walked out on stage – I was opening the show. It was after a long European tour, I'd been over there about three months, and to me it was just another show and get the hell home. And when I walked out on stage, Christ, the place just went crazy! There were banners that said "Welcome back Bill Haley".

'We did a show and they marched in the aisles and out in the streets and stopped the show cold and I just stood up there and cried, because there was no time in my life that I was ever more down musically. So we did about an hour and a half and stopped the show cold, and that spread all over show business, what had happened. And we were in Amsterdam after that, we played there and the same thing happened.'

Upon Haley's return to England for another tour in 1968 he was given a hero's welcome. 'Scores of leather-clad young rockers turned out to greet their ancestral hero, Bill Haley, when he flew in from America yesterday', wrote a reporter for the *Daily Mirror*. In the press photos Haley appeared stunned by the reception, which featured a wildly supportive crowd carrying placards reading 'Welcome Back Bill Haley' and 'Rock Forever'. He was wreathed with flowers by adoring fans and presented with a huge mocked-up record with the garish inscription: 'Welcome Back To Britain Bill Haley King Of Rock 'N' Roll Forever.' One fan told reporters at the scene 'I've got all his records. How could people have possibly liked the Beatles when there's always been Bill Haley?'

On May 2nd a mixture of old Teddy boys and new Rockers came out in force for Haley's concert at the Albert Hall in London. The crowd booed the opening act, the Quotations, whose drummer was beaned with a flying bottle. Duane Eddy didn't fare much better until he played his old hits. When Haley hit the stage he told the crowd 'You don't know how happy you've made me tonight,' but his joy was gone half an hour later when he fled part of the way through 'Rock Around the Clock' as the crowd spilled onto the stage. Emcee Rick Dane stayed around long enough to be kicked by the fans and dragged offstage before he was rescued by security guards.

Haley's appeal obviously hadn't dimmed, and by the time his three week tour of England was completed 'Rock Around the Clock' had returned to the top of the singles charts in that country.

'At first I didn't really believe that rock could come back,' Haley said during the tour, 'but now I'm not sure. The interest in beat music which the Beatles created has now died down. We are in a lull. The music has slowed, and the freshness has been taken out of it. There are too many branch ideas, like the psychedelic cult, which don't give the kids anything to dance to. No one else is left playing rock & roll the way it was originated, and that's why the demand started for me. I don't feel myself it was a demand for me personally. I have never been a sex symbol. Nor have any of my band, the Comets. We don't sell sex or looks. We simply have a style of music which pleases people and still has them stomping and clapping for us.'

After another successful European tour in 1969, Haley started a rock & roll revival back in the U.S. in the fall of the same year. He headlined Richard Nader's '50s revival package show so successfully that he topped a similar program a little more than a month later. The response was awesome. Fans nostalgic for '50s rock came out of the woodwork, and the critical reaction was surprisingly favorable. Mike John wrote in *The New York Times* 'They played with great energy and talent, making a relatively simple, shuffling style sound as exciting as almost anything heard lately.'

For his part, Haley was ecstatic with his revived success. 'It's not been an easy road,' he said, 'to stick with what we were doing, to be labelled as a has-been. We could have changed our styles a long time ago but we stuck with it. When I'm seventy-five, if I can still play the guitar, I'll still play rock & roll.'

139

Nineteen: Rock Around the Country

DURING THE HEIGHT of Haley's European revival he began his association with Sonet Records in Sweden, the company which released his last seven LPs. At the end of a spectacularly successful Swedish tour in 1968, Sonet's president, Dag Heckses, persuaded Haley to record for the company. Haley cut two live albums for Sonet in front of enthusiastic studio audiences. The sets included rock & roll material sung by different members of the group – guitarist Nick Nastos singing 'Whole Lotta Shakin' Goin' On', bassist Al Rappa singing 'Lucille' and Swedish singer Gert Lengstrand on 'What'd I Say'.

At the same time Haley made a third record for Sonet, *Biggest Hits*, an earnest but not particularly historic set of re-recorded favorites like 'Rock Around the Clock', 'See You Later Alligator', 'Skinny Minnie', 'Shake Rattle and Roll' etc. The Sonet Records sold well on the European market, but the first three LPs pretty much exhausted their ideas for him. Haley, of course, suggested they let him record an album of country songs. In fact he'd cut a fairly good country song in the U.S. for United Artists, a version of the Tom T. Hall tune 'That's How I Got to Memphis', so the idea had its appeal.

In 1970 Sonet added the brilliant young American producer Sam Charters to their staff. Charters, a scholar and musicologist as well as a producer, had put together an interesting series of LPs while working for Prestige and Vanguard records as well as several authoritative books on Memphis-based blues artists. Having produced such esoteric acts as Country Joe and the Fish and the Holy Modal Rounders as well as a number of blues albums, Sonet's first assignment to Charters, to produce a country album with Haley in Nashville, came as a bit of a shock.

'When I decided that I wanted to leave the United States,'

140

says Charters, 'I knew of Sonet because I met them when I had been over there with Country Joe and the Fish. They said "Fine, come over, but the first thing we want you to do is Bill Haley in the United States before you come." Considering that I had been with Country Joe in San Francisco, I thought it was so startling tnat they suggested it. But at the same time I regarded it as a very exciting challenge. Bill was performing a lot in those days and was around the United States, and I knew it would be possible for me to work with him in a personal way. It was the period of the rock & roll revival and Bill's name was around a fair bit, and he was actually in the United States performing with a live band, really doing kind of extended tours, motels and small clubs.'

It was at one of these clubs that Charters first met Haley. 'Bill was at this club on East 79th Street in New York City, there they were up on the stage in this small club really giving it their all, performing like it was a huge stadium. They were filling the place with their personality and energy, and it seemed on the one hand incredibly incongruous that they were doing it, but at the same time they did it well. When they went into their routines with all of them dancing on the stage together, the kind of unison dance steps that they did, it was just a knock-out.

'Bill and I sat between sets and talked quite a bit, and as he said later "I didn't really know what you thought about the music. I just wanted to know if I could work with you, you son-of-a-bitch." We spent a lot of time together that night, and then I went down to Washington to be with the band on the weekend, and they were just playing motels. Most of the gigs were dance music and country ballads that the band played, and then Bill came out and they did a set of old Comets favorites.'

Charters was fascinated by the ageing pop star and quickly befriended Haley. 'At the first meeting it was so bizarre,' Charters recalls. 'Bill had just gone into the mango business, and he bought this large plot of land in the state of Vera Cruz in Mexico and he was going to plant 300 acres of mangos. What we talked about mostly were his mangos and the problems he had had because the land he bought was right in the way of a cattle trail that the local land owners had been using for many, many years to drive their cattle across. Bill was going to fence it off and put in mangos. So he actually had pistoleros riding

141

around his land driving off his ranch hands and coming up on the steps of the porch and saying "Mr. Haley, we have been doing this for years," and flashing their pistols.

'It wasn't until we really got to know each other and I saw him in the studio and I saw his real uncertainty about what to do next that I realized what an unhappy man he was. Then finally I realized that in the time I knew him the only time he was really happy was when he was singing 'Rock Around the Clock'.

Charters' first production with Haley, *Rock Around the Country*, was an artistic triumph but a commercial failure. 'It's always difficult to work with an artist whose career is not going,' says Charters. 'You don't know really whether to continue the old direction or try something new. And Bill himself could never decide. Usually at the last moment he opted out and sort of scurried back to what he knew he could do and what he knew was successful.'

Rock Around the Country was Haley's only departure from the style of his Decca classics that really worked musically. It was a compromise between Haley's desire to revive his country roots and Charters' concern with bringing his sound up to date. 'On Bill's side there was continual belief that if he were to sing country ballads that would be his breakthrough,' Charters points out. 'There was always a continual stream of suggestions about ballads, about country songs, about country and western material from Bill. It was very close to his heart. He recognized, in a way, that he had reached a dead end in what he was doing, and he was looking around for new things to do.

'I didn't believe there was any hope for Bill Haley singing country and western ballads. Bill's voice is a high voice, it's kind of a light voice, and the great country singers have a much heavier voice. Bill had a wonderful boyish cheerfulness with that voice, and I couldn't see him doing the kind of ballads he wanted to do.'

So Haley got to do ballads like 'There's a New Moon Over My Shoulder,' 'I Wouldn't Have Missed It for the World' and 'A Little Piece At a Time.' In exchange Charters got him to record songs like 'Games People Play' and 'Who'll Stop the Rain.' According to Charters, 'the most important one for me was "Me and Bobby McGee". The most important one for him was "A Little Piece At a Time". When the record did come out in the

142

United States it was a disaster. Bill hired a personal publicity man to push "A Little Piece At a Time" at the same time we were pushing to get a single of "Me and Bobby McGee". So we just had complete cross-purposes.'

Charters got Haley to sing material he was completely unfamiliar with on this record. 'Bill was particularly dubious about "Me and Bobby McGee",' says Charters. 'He just didn't think he could do that one at all. Bill was really thrown by these songs. He just didn't know how to deal with his voice at all. Once he committed himself to doing the songs Bill worked hard. When he decided he was going to sing a song he sang that song over and over and over and over and over until he got a way that worked for him.'

Charters maintained that Haley's high quality performance on that record was due to the fact that he'd been working steadily. 'He was singing regularly with a band and the core musicians on the album are the band he was traveling with. We added Nashville people to it, but they were very much added. Rudy Pompilli was in absolute top form. After that Bill seemed sort of out of it. They were all scuffling around Chester, Pa., in the bars and Nashville in the bars while Bill was in Mexico running his fishing boat or building his hotel or raising his mangos.'

Charters attempted to stay in contact with Haley in order to get him back into the studio, but it would take three years before the follow-up album was made. 'We were always planning new records. But with his other interests and with the complications of his life in Mexico, it was very hard to get him into the studio. We'd spend months gathering material then he'd cancel at the last minute.

'His situation was so confused in Mexico,' Charters explains. 'His life just kept changing and shifting and he had troubles with the band, troubles with the tours, troubles with his managers, and he just couldn't get anything going in Mexico. The mangos didn't work. We would get calls from him, he would want a quick advance to put an elevator in his hotel. So we were selling records pretty steadily around the world, no big hits but still steady sales, so sure, we would advance him the money for the elevator. Then he could never get the hotel open. Then he had the fishing boat and it was only one fishing boat and he had to take the fishing tours out from there. Martha, his wife, had a large family and Bill was supporting them, and so he would get ready to record and then there would be some incredible catastrophe within this confused network of things he was trying to do in Mexico, or else he was coming to work as part of a tour, and then the tour would collapse because it was badly planned. And Bill himself was unreliable.'

Charters referred to what at that point was Haley's massive drinking problem. It led to problems, but it was something Sam was used to. 'I had started out with jazz musicians Bill's age so I was very used to drinking as being one of the problems. I was in Chicago with the Muddy Waters Band, not Muddy himself, but all the guys in Chicago drank. Drinking was not new to me. The problem with Bill was that everything depended on him and it wasn't the kind of thing he could do when he was drunk. He is not like Jerry Lee Lewis.'

Haley had other illnesses that disrupted his touring and recording schedule and was rumored in 1972 to have suffered a heart attack. His rollercoaster existence was typified by the two most important events in Haley's life during '72, his show-stealing performance at the Wembley rock & roll revival and the massive lawsuit slapped on him by his longtime booking agent, Jolly Joyce, which would have jeopardized any money Haley earned at home for concert appearances.

Joyce wasn't the only creditor looking to attach Haley's box office receipts. 'He was playing a date in Lancaster a few years ago and the Bell Telephone slapped a lien on,' says booking agent Jim Feddis. And then there was the time Haley got cold feet before the rock & roll revival show in Philadelphia and blew the gig. His oldest son and a number of friends had gone to see Haley's triumphant return to the Chester area only to find out that Bill could not go through with it. 'From the day I said goodbye to Bill I ain't never seen him since,' says Ralph Jones. 'I went up one night to the Spectrum to see the revival rock & roll show he was on. I went back to the dressing room and Rudy says "Eh Ralph, forget it. He's over in New Jersey bombed out, he won't be here." Jack cried like a baby. He brought his friends there to meet his father and he didn't show.'

The making of Haley's 1973 album, *Just Rock and Roll Music*, was a nightmare for everyone concerned. Charters' difficulties began before Haley even made it to the sessions. 'He made himself hard to reach,' explains Charters. 'I had to go through the brother in Mexico City. It was hopeless to call from Stockholm to Mexico City to try to speak with somebody in Spanish, then trying to reach Bill in Vera Cruz. I never knew whether the telegram would get through. Suddenly telegrams would come back to me that had no relationship to what I was trying to say.

'It was so difficult to tell with Bill whether he had gotten the word or whether he was gone off on another one of his side trips emotionally, so it was always just havoc. And as difficult as it was for me, it was much harder for the band, because they had to be ready to drop their lives and take off when Bill called. Rudy always had to be there at the beck and call.'

Pompilli's faithful service to Haley had been strained to its limits. Ralph Jones heard some hair raising stories. 'All I know is when Rudy came home we'd get together and talk and it was always bad. The guy was drinking, it was a bad scene, the money was bad, half the time he didn't get paid. He owed Rudy a *lot* of money, I know it.'

Haley's drinking was a particularly divisive element because Rudy hardly ever drank himself. 'The band was kind of split,' says Charters 'because one or two of them were drinking, the bass player was always called in for late night drinks. But the rest of the band didn't drink so much. So there wasn't this kind of happy comraderie, "Let's go down to the bar and get stewed." Bill would sort of slip off with the bass player and the band would be waiting for them to get back.'

Charters observed that the long-term effects of Haley's behavior on Pompilli were terrible. 'There obviously had been ten or fifteen years of this long standing sadness,' he points out, 'or perhaps disappointment is a better word. He hadn't been able to go on with his career as a jazz musician. He dropped off from being *Downbeat's* most promising baritone sax player of the year to playing out-of-tune tenor, loud rock & roll. He was proud of what he did in a way, deeply proud of it. But he was also deeply ashamed of it, and so he did have the clarinet with him in the dressing rooms, and he would sit there at night by himself and play Artie Shaw tunes, and Benny Goodman tunes, and felt very sorry for himself. There was a residue of anger

145

toward Bill because of this.

'Rudy would put up with things in Bill that none of the rest of us would. He was incredibly trusting, incredibly loving, incredibly gentle. When they would play these God awful country clubs, and you can imagine what they were like fifteen years ago before anyone was into country music. And Rudy had this very nice little house that he was very proud of, and these guys in the band would bring back a God awful chick, and leave bloody sheets and bottles all over the floor and leave Rudy to clean it up. Them skanky broads, as Rudy used to put it. It's a word you don't hear often.'

When Haley arrived in Nashville for the *Just Rock and Roll* sessions, it was obvious to Charters that Haley's drinking had escalated past the danger point. 'Haley was just staggeringly drunk all of the time,' says Charters, 'and I never really had any idea, literally from one moment to the next whether the session was just going to blow up in my face. Bill was really, really difficult. It was the worst I ever saw him when I was working with him.'

Charters recalled that Haley's personal life was particularly confused at that point. 'When we were staying at the motel together before we did *Just Rock and Roll Music* he told me a long, rambling story about the land he bought for the hotel in Vera Cruz. He said without knowing it he bought a plot of land that had been wanted by the syndicate in Mexico, and they had threatened him and his family, and he had beaten up a guy, and he was afraid, just physically afraid. This was hanging over him. Also there was the incredible confusion between Patrick Malynn and Jolly Joyce, his management and booking agent. There were just continual hassles and struggles, and Bill felt himself very alone in all of this.'

As the sessions progressed Charters realized he was dealing with a hopeless case. Haley was so out of it Charters had to point him toward the microphone when he sang.

'He had no idea where it was and suddenly he began having these splitting headaches, miserable headaches, because of the drinking. At that point Haley was a very unhappy man. That's what he talked about most, the money and the difficulties financially that he had been having. I think he had had very high hopes at the first record we had done. He worked very hard in

146

thinking about the songs and he went along with me. When it hadn't come to much he was very disappointed, and yet he realized that his best chance was to stay with Sonet. But still he was a difficult fellow.'

Charters made the best of it, even building a party scene into the end of the remake of 'Crazy Man, Crazy'. The Nashville session crew was not particularly concerned with Haley's behavior. 'It's a heavy drinking city,' says Charters. 'A lot of them drink themselves. They come and open the guitar case and put the bottle beside it and they do it from Monday morning to Friday night.' At one point in the sessions, country singer Donna Fargo came to watch Haley perform. 'She came in to see Bill, who was her idol,' says Charters. 'I remember her standing just quietly in the control room beside me looking at him, really, really honored. Standing silently watching this man carry on'.

Haley's wild drunkenness reached its climax on the last day of the session. 'I kept trying to get him in the studio fairly straight. So I would sit there not drinking with him trying to keep him from drinking. But it was the last day when we were on our way to the studio to do the last songs and some vocals, we were just getting there and it looked pretty good. Bill said "Oh, there is one more thing that I want to tell you." And in the three minutes it took him to tell me this meaningless thing he had to tell me he managed to get down three more whiskey and sodas. He signalled to the waitress and she kept handing him the things. Right in the middle of a sentence, zip, down would go a drink, so he was absolutely plowed when he got to the studio.

'It had been building the whole time. He was just feeling all the pressures of his past life. He was feeling poor. Everything came down on him, and he got steadily, steadily drunker and more morose and belligerent as sessions went on. He got down those three quick whiskey and sodas and he was just impossible. Just impossible. He couldn't see the microphone.'

They wrapped up the record and returned to the motel, where Haley proceeded to have a breakdown for a full day. 'It was most of the day and night and the next morning,' Charters recalls. 'He tended to get very mean and ugly toward the band. I was sort of exempted from it, but it got real . . . "You son of a bitch! You are nothing! I made you!" And he started to get very violent with them and he would break furniture and carry on. So

147

the band was locked in their rooms. They locked themselves in and left Bill roaming the corridors at the motel. I was just trying to keep everybody calmed down and get Bill on his way back to Mexico. The motel people called me and said "Look, if this weren't Bill Haley we would have the police in and have him arrested." I said "Yes." And they said "In this town we try to look after idols. It isn't the first time it happens, but it is always the last time it happens. Don't you ever bring Bill Haley back to Nashville again." '

So Haley was run out of Nashville in disgrace. 'Bill idolized Nashville and Nashville musicians, and he felt very, very badly about carrying on so. And there were always promises, extravagant promises when he sobered up. He was a classic, classic drunk. A lot of extravagant promises, and sadly enough there were promises that he would share a little financially with Rudy. And when Rudy was getting the chemo-therapy treatments they were costing him a fortune, and Bill didn't help, Rudy just excused him.'

Rudy Pompilli was stricken by lung cancer during a 1974 European tour. At first it was thought he just had flu, but when the band returned to the States Rudy learned the tragic news. Rudy's final wish was to record his own album, and Charters made arrangements for Haley to meet up with Rudy and the Comets one last time. 'My recollection is that despite everything we were going to try Nashville a third time. Bill was supposed to meet us there, and we had to cancel it.

'That was the incredible awful time when I was sitting there in the motel with the band and with Rudy, waiting for Bill to show up. And he just drank his way up the east coast of Mexico. I did get the calls from the bartenders saying "Senor Haley has just hit a policeman. He is on his way." Then finally Bill called from the border when he reached Texas three days late, he had no voice and he said "I can't talk. I can't sing." He couldn't do it. Then he told me afterwards, a long time afterwards, that he just couldn't face Rudy dying.'

Even at that terrible moment Pompilli showed compassion for his old friend. 'We left the other guys up in the motel and went down to have some coffee and talk about what to do next,' Charters recalls, 'because the plan was that Bill was going to do an album and Rudy would do a solo album with Bill backing him up. Rudy felt sorry for Bill saying "He had this long drive, the band has broken up, he doesn't know what to do with his career, I am dying."

'He was in very bad shape. He was going to make this album with Bill backing him up because he dreamed of this for some years. I liked Rudy, I felt I had committed myself to Rudy and I said there's gonna be a record, no matter what. We had a whole repertory worked out if Bill was going to do it. Then we had to stop, go back and start all over again and use local musicians that Rudy had been working with himself. So it turned out to be a different kind of a record. Sadly enough the musicians weren't right. He knew it and I knew it and they knew it. The musicians really loved Rudy. I remember in the control room they all brought their girl friends and their wives. Their wives would say "Rudy is dying isn't he? We feel so sad. We love him so much." He was that kind of person.

'My last recollection is Rudy sitting in the back room which he had turned into a musician's den, there were all the records he had made, and there were pictures of him playing with Duke Ellington, pictures of the Comets. He completely accepted his death. So my recollection is of him sitting in that room talking one more time about the Comets. He was pleased that they had done so much, even though he didn't quite understand why it happened.'

Rock 'revival' tonight at 8

NOV 21 1971

Chuck Berry, Bo Diddley, The Shirelles, The Dovells, Gary U. S. Bonds and Bill Haley and his Comets are the headliners for the "Rock & Roll Revival" show scheduled for 8 tonight at the Seattle Center Arena.

The show is sponsored by Northwest Releasing and is designed to create nostalgia for the rock and roll sounds of the 1950s.

Haley's Comets at Raceway

JUL 11 1974

Bill Haley and the Comets will appear in the Olympia Nitro Jam Saturday night at Seattle International Raceway.

Haley's outdoor show at 10 p.m. will follow a day of drag-racing at the Raceway, on Highway 18 east of Kent.

Twenty: The End

RUDY POMPILLI COULD not be replaced. Without the advice and support of the man who had been the heart of the Comets, Haley was left rudderless. Bill bravely tried to go on with the sessions for his next album without Rudy. It was torture, even in the planning stages when the usual problem of material came up. 'The problem with Bill was to get the right material,' says Charters, 'so I spent months and months and months every year listening to new songs, old songs, trying to get songs. In Nashville we went down publishers' row asking if anyone had a song for us. Bill's kind of songs were so unique and there was really no one else doing Bill's kind of songs in the '70s.'

'Bill had a sense of the kind of thing he could do. It wasn't so much of a formula, but you had to find something that was uptempo, cheerful, optimistic, didn't make much sense, and there couldn't be anything sexual in what Bill did. That was what was so strange about it. He was essentially an unerotic rock & roll singer. So love songs didn't work, sort of uptempo "Hey baby I'm gonna do something or other" — that never worked. It had to be about a party because his voice was particularly effective for this one thing but it didn't work for a lot of things.'

So Haley ended up making another album of remakes of his Decca material. Ironically, several of the songs were from the end of Haley's Decca era when he was desperately floundering around looking to recapture the vitality of his original sound. 'I Got a Woman', 'Farewell, So Long, Goodbye' and even 'Ooh! Look-A There Ain't She Pretty' do come off pretty well. Haley stayed straight for this album, *R-O-C-K*, and worked hard on it. 'Bill was himself in pretty good shape,' recalled Charters. 'He brought Martha and his boy. They drove up all the way from

150

Mexico. Martha was from a very strong, very close Mexican family that had had its troubles ... she knew about drinking. Knew how to keep Bill close. So he wasn't drinking, but he was so subdued after the death of Rudy. And his voice lowered slightly, and things had to be put in lower keys for him. But he wasn't the Bill Haley he had been when we made *Rock Around the Country*.

'There was a great question whether he would continue at all,' Charters notes of Haley's reaction to Pompilli's death. 'When we came to Muscle Shoals and it was necessary to continue with a different saxophone player it was shattering. Bill and I would just sit there waiting for Rudy to come in. Waiting for Rudy to make his solos, help us with the arrangements. He wasn't there. And it was almost impossible for this guy to try to fit in Rudy's shoes. He realized immediately what was going on. We finally had to re-do all the parts.

'Also, Bill never had the rapport with the Muscle Shoals musicians like he did with the Nashville musicians. He felt, always, that there was a tug between what he wanted to do and what they did. So finally we wanted to finish up the album with something that they wanted to do. So we kind of talked it over, and everyone decided to do "Mohair Sam" and we did the first run-down and Bill turned to me and said "So now we know what they do".'

A reluctant Haley was persuaded by Patrick Malynn to attempt some more live shows, but the results were disastrous. On December 3, 1976, at the London Victoria Theatre, Haley's show was interrupted right at the start by anarchic fighting between Teddy Boys and bouncers which continued sporadically throughout the performance and resulted in a number of arrests. 'There were quite a few broken noses,' says a fan who attended the show, 'and geezers were coming out of the orchestra pit with blood pouring from their faces. It made that punk rock lark look like a kids' nursery'.

Haley was disconsolate about playing without Rudy, and called Pompilli's wife, Ann, for solace. 'He said "They can't put another horn player in Rudy's place," ' Ann recalls. ' "I can't play with these clowns." That's the way he was. He didn't mean to be nasty. It was very hard for that man to try to take on somebody new.'

Haley proceeded to go into retirement. He refused to perform in public or to record for almost three years, splitting his time between stays at his Mexico home and in Texas. The obscurity of life in those parts is what appealed to him. 'I've been living down there on and off for fifteen years,' he said in 1979. 'I like Mexico. I like the place, I like the Spanish instead of English . . . it's a place to get away from it all. Man, down here they don't know nothing. They don't know from nothing or care — especially the Spanish. It's a home. It's not a big deal. I'm a very conservative guy, not one of those millionaires. I'm not a Presley type guy.'

In 1979 Haley returned to activity. 'I was out of the business for the past three years,' he explained, 'because my saxophone player died. We were together for twenty-five years, and we had a pact, if he died first, I would stop playing, and if I died first, he would not play. But now I feel the mourning period is over, and I'm about eighty per cent ready to go back on the road.

'It was quite a shock when Rudy got cancer,' he continued. 'We did a tour of Brazil, and I could see him failing. I knew he was going, and I couldn't face it. I thought every time I'd walk out on the stage and look out on my right or on my left that he wouldn't be there. And I did lean heavily on the guy. So consequently when he passed away I remembered and I said that was it and I just quit it.

'For a year, I wouldn't even consider it (playing again). I didn't want to listen to records, I wouldn't hear music or anything. And I really went into hiding. I wouldn't tell anybody I was Bill Haley. I lived in Mexico and I went fishing and just got away from it, you know. And gradually, little by little, I began to think. Here he and I had worked twenty-five years and we had created something. I started talking to people and they said "This is not right. You've devoted your life to giving music to people." And then last year Elvis died. I guess Elvis was kind of a cushion for me, because whatever he did made headlines everywhere and he kept the name alive and what have you. Then after he passed away, I started to see all these movies coming out and I thought "Well, if I don't start to come back and speak for it, why, there's not really any leader left or anybody to keep the interest there." '

Haley's determination to pick up the flag of '50s rock & roll after Presley had fallen is in keeping with his career-long interest to promote rock & roll culture as he knew it in the '50s. But his campaign failed and his remaining efforts were sadly inadequate attempts to recontact his muse. In March of '79 he toured England to mixed reviews although he did provide another platform for fans of his era's music. 'Punk is too high class,' a fifteen-year-old complained to the *Evening Standard*. 'It started out as music for kids but it soon became too tied up in the fashion world. And it never had the same beat as rock & roll.'

Haley's last album, *Everyone Can Rock & Roll,* was recorded during the summer of 1979 at Fame Studios in Muscle Shoals. Under the direction of British producer Kenny Denton, an enthusiastic band of southern rockers tried to contemporize Haley in a style markedly different from that used by the various versions of the Comets. The idea had its merits – Haley's original sound actually had a lot in common with '70s southern rock. 'Juke Box Cannonball', which Haley had recorded thirty years earlier with the Saddlemen, came out pretty well, as did a few other numbers on the record. Unfortunately, though, the album failed to revive Haley's musical energies in any serious way.

Strange reports about Haley were circulating during '79. During his tour of England and Europe later in the year something was apparently wrong with him. He was reported to have kicked fans, taken off his clothes onstage and thrown a microphone stand into the audience. This was in fact pretty tame show business behavior compared to what some of the punk bands were doing at the same time. And Haley certainly was aware of punk rock's theatrics. 'They're just trying to create an image,' he said of punk rockers. 'Those guys aren't as bad as all that.'

Unfortunately, Haley's version of punk rock stagings didn't go over as well as his previous approaches, and by 1980, when he suddenly cancelled another tour of England and Europe, rumors of his impending death began to circulate. In the October 25, 1980 edition of the German paper *Bild,* Haley's German tour manager, Wolfgang Burch, commented on the cancellation of that month's tour 'He can never play his guitar again. Never again be able to sing his wild songs.'

The report stated that Haley had a brain tumor. British

manager Patrick Malynn was quoted as saying 'In recent times he was often in the hospital, but at the beginning of tours he was always fit; this time no. For that reason I sent a man to him in the clinic in Los Angeles. Bill Haley spoke to the man so: "Hey, there you are, finally." Then he let himself be brought to his villa in Beverley Hills. Three hours later, he suddenly took a fit and went over the seat. He didn't recognize anyone anymore. Back to the clinic. A doctor said "The tumor can't be operated on anymore." The tumor could well be the cause of Haley's wild actions onstage.'

A few days later another paper, the *Berliner Zeitung*, reported that Haley was undergoing a 'cold turkey' alcoholism cure. 'The man who became world famous with his cowlick and plaid jacket collapsed after a concert in Texas with a collapse of his circulatory system. He was immediately transported into the hospital of his home town, Harlingen, in Texas. The physicians ascertained that the cause was the huge consumption of alcohol by the singer. For that reason he was ordered to take a cure.

'The doctors are convinced,' the report went on, 'that Bill Haley will soon have finished his cure. Given the circumstances his state of health is not such that he is in danger of dying.'

Twenty-One: Crazy Man, Crazy

BILL HALEY'S FINAL public appearances were in South Africa in May and June, 1980, a sad tour in which the dying rock star was heavily criticized in the press for his poor showing. Haley returned to his final home in Harlingen, Texas, to die.

His last sorrowful days on earth have left a confusing but indelible mark. Towards the end of his life he made a succession of tortured late night phone calls to distant friends and relatives in the Chester/Philadelphia area, an elaborate spiritual pilgrimage to his roots, one last time before he died. His phone calls were bizarre conversations, mostly monologues in which Bill seemed to his interlocutors either incoherently drunk or ill.

Dorothy Haley, his first wife, remembers the calls. 'He would keep me on the phone two or three hours in the wee hours of the morning,' she says. 'He would call and ramble and dwell on the past, his mind was really warped . . . Oh, it used to tear me up but I couldn't hang up on him. You don't hang up when someone is sick.'

Haley liked to call Rudy Pompilli's wife Ann and reminisce, even though he'd never actually met her. 'Bill called me many times,' Annie says. 'When he called me it wasn't at regular hours. He called me at like three o'clock in the morning, four a.m., and he'd be on the phone for an hour, an hour and a half at a time.

'He was a sick man. I had talked to Martha and she told me. He was a funny man too. He would say he was calling from Scotland and he was having dinner with the Queen. He would tease me. He'd call me Ann Queen of Scotland. I said "Bill, don't start. You're such a horse's ass!" He'd say "Don't you believe I'm here with Lizzy?" He was funny, he used to tease me all the time. When Rudy told him we were getting married he

155

called me up and he says "I'm calling to check you out." I said "You do what you like. I really don't care, I'm not marrying you." He said "You'd better be good to my brother," he always called Rudy his brother. I said "Yeah and if I'm not?" He says "I'll be up there!" I said "Unhuh! You scare me."

'And I never met that man,' Ann marvels. 'He'd tease me all the time. He would sing to me. There was many a time when he'd call me up at that hour and he would cry. And all he'd talk about was Rudy.'

The calls weren't all singing and crying and reminiscing, though. Haley's calls to former and present business associates were often belligerent.

Rex Zario is one of the people Haley called frequently in his last year. Zario had done the same country and western circuit as Haley at roughly the same time, recording for Jack Howard. In 1954 Zario's biggest hit, the regional breakout 'Go Man Go Get Gone', was released on Arcade. After Jack Howard died Zario inherited his interest in Haley's early publishing, and leased some of the Saddlemen sides to an Australian record company which released them in LP form. Zario sent Haley checks, using the last available Mexican address, but never knew if the royalties reached their intended destination. Months later Zario got a late night phone call from Haley, the first in a series of calls that were so bizarre Zario decided to tape them.

Zario lives in one of a row of wooden houses in a poor section of North Philadelphia. A quiet man with an interest in horse racing (his kitchen table is covered with five-year-old racing forms), Zario worked in Dave Miller's pressing plant and knows the history of the Philadelphia music scene from the inside. Jimmy Myers, who also owns the rights to some of Haley's existing material, talked of putting together new packages of Haley material controlled by himself and Zario. The material in Zario's archives is a meticulous collection of paraphernalia from the era, from Saddlemen performance contracts to boxes of pressing plant labels, but of all the Haley-ana he owns, Zario is proudest of a demo tape Haley recorded for Milt Gabler called 'Football Rock & Roll'.

Zario's living room consists of a few chairs, a shelf of records, his sound system and two tape recorders which dominate the setting. The tapes of Haley's phone calls fill the room as he sits, smoking menthol cigarettes, staring at the floor. . . .

Haley: Now I'm playing a tape for you if you'll wait. Now I want you to hear something. I got a tape recorder here that I'm rewinding while you're talking. What time is it in Philadelphia? It must be about 11:30 at night?

Zario: Yes it is. 11:30 on the dot.

Haley: All right. I'm calling you from Harlingen, Texas. I'm telling you, friend, that I got a son named Scott Haley. All right you know all that *jive* don't you Jack.

Zario: Yeh, I don't know him but you told me about him before.

Haley: I'm going to have Captain Buddy Larimore, the Chief of Police call you 'cause now I got your number but you don't want to listen do you? I got a lawyer in Philadelphia. I got several lawyers in Philadelphia. I got a lawyer and I whipped Norman George, and oh yeah, you know *everything* don't you Rex Zario. Now you hang in there *friend* cos I'm gonna play you something that's gonna teach you a fucking lesson and I know who ASCAP is and I got all the things on Valleybrook and you tell me about that six-foot-seven guy that owns my publishing company. Now you hang in with me just a second on this toll free line, it's rewinding, wait 'till it stops, now hang in with me cos I'm rewinding the tape here. Now just wait . . . this tape recording as seen at the Bitter End in New York City all right?

Zario: All right. I got the record.

Haley: You *do*, huh? Well. . . .

Zario: I got all your records.

Haley: You do? Well let's see if you got *this* one. Wait. You got 'em all.

Zario: I got 'em all. I got all your records.

Haley: Well, let's see if you *do*. Now wait. Wait, now.

Zario: I'm here.

Haley: Do you remember George Jones?

Zario: Yeah. 'White Lightning' and all that.

Haley: How about 'She Thinks I Still Care?' Do you remember that one?

Zario: I got that record.

Haley: Have you got one by Bill Haley in Spanish?

157

Zario: No, I didn't know you had recorded that.

Haley: Here, now this is Bill Haley singing . . . (music) No wait, let me run it ahead a little bit. You got all my records. Now wait, I got a change of pace here for you, *friend.*

Zario: In fact I even got a record you did of 'Football Rock & Roll'.

Haley: Wait a minute now. (His version of 'She Thinks I Still Care' plays over the phone. Haley sings drunkenly along with the recording.) 'Just because you think la da dee dee . . . She thinks I still ca-a-a-are.'

Zario: (also singing) 'She thinks I still care.'

Haley: Now listen.

Zario: All right. I can hear it a little bit.

Haley: Now you tell me I don't sing in *Spanish,* you asshole.

Zario: That's good, Bill. That one I don't have.

Haley: You tell me I didn't have the biggest Mexican record in Mexico called (pause, he seems to forget what he was talking about) Now you see I collect royalties from Mexico, too, *friend,* cos I sing in the two languages.

Zario: I don't blame you.

Haley: You got all them records don't you. Let me run it ahead a little bit, *friend.* Now, shit, I run it backwards now because you know so much. I'm gonna break all these tapes 'cos you got a big mouth up in Philadelphia. Now if you'll just hang in with me, I'm spending a lot of money to play these for you today. I'm gonna give you the full treatment. . . .

(The tape is rolled ahead.)

Haley: And I'm *paying* for this call. I want you to just be kind enough to let me pay for it, and don't let me break my tape. I'm looking at what it says: Bill Haley 'Jealous Heart' Country Songs Spanish/English (forcefully) Who's Freddy Fender, all right?

Zario: I'm listening.

Haley: Well, why don't you *listen* and let me rewind the tape and shut your *mouth* and then, all right now do I stop it now, or do you want to know who *Freddy Fender* is?

(Tape fast forward again.)

Haley: I don't wanna break this tape because you got everything recorded, and you'll send me another copy of this one. Are you listening?

158

Zario: I'm listening. ('Shake Rattle & Roll' plays on the tape.)

Haley: Now Rex, Martha and I are divorced and I don't have my little daughter any more, my five-year-old daughter, here in Harlingen, Texas. Now I want you to be a witness for me, you listen to what I'm telling you.

Zario: Yeah.

Haley: Two times they told you there was a warrant out for my arrest.

Zario: Yeah.

Haley: The third time you asked them, now somehow you called and when you recorded them they said there wasn't.

Zario: Right. There was no warrant out.

Haley: All right now, that's the third time you called.

Zario: Right, because the last time I called for the night jail, remember?

Haley: Do I *remember?* Do I remember, *pal!* You know what time it is? Quarter to two in the morning and I'm still here.

Zario: I know and you're sober too.

Haley: I'm sober as a judge. You know where the judge is? You wanna talk to the judge?

(A garbled exchange follows.)

Haley: I'm calling you back and I'm asking you to be a witness for me, I'm gonna have Captain Buddy Larimore to call you and if you want his fucking phone number I'm gonna give it to you and you call him and tell him what you just heard. Then he's gonna ask you how you got his fucking phone number and then you *are* gonna be in jail! No but (mimics Zario's voice) oh oh fuck, oh piss, oh shit, I just took another piss I must be . . . ohhh! WILL YOU LET ME FUCKING TALK YOU ASSHOLE? Are you gonna fucking listen?

Haley: But you can't keep your fucking mouth shut!

Zario: All right I won't say anything until you ask me.

Haley: Will you hang the fucking phone up if you . . . let me talk, why don't you quit talking about me and realize that I love you . . .

(Long silence.)

Haley: Now *that's* the way you and me talk.

(Silence)

Haley: That's a beautiful conversation ... Now twice you called Harlingen police station.

Zario: No. three times.

Haley: Three times! Four times! Seven times! Aw, go fuck yourself. You can't keep your mouth shut. (pause) Seventeen times you called ... nineteen times you called, ninety-seven times. . . and you want to talk. Now I'll tell you what, go fuck yourself! Now *you* talk.

Zario: I don't know what to say.

Haley: Where's Jimmy Myers? (pause) Where's Buddy Larimore? (pause) He's in Sicily. (Mimics Rex) 'I've been listening Bill, cos I'm tough from Philadelphia. I'm afraid to call down there, you might check me out.' Now I wanna hit you with one and I wanna show you the mafia, alright? *Now* you'll keep your mouth shut, won't you? Cause I'm gonna give you a number in Miami Beach and *he'll* shut your mouth. I seem to carry a little more weight tonight than I did, don't I? Now I'm not gonna hit you with any names, friend. You know *everything*, don't you? I'll give you some more names, now, you wanna write em down?

(Haley reads off a series of names.)

Haley: I'm going to tell you something you little son of a bitch.

Zario: See you don't listen to me, I have to listen to you.

Haley: I have to fucking listen to you because all you're doing is 'Don't drink, Bill.' 'I feel sorry for you Bill.' Now I'm gonna *tell* you because I don't *back* down and you better fucking listen to me. You are *stupid*.

Zario: Yeah, 'cos you said I'm stupid. Well, you're right. I wish I was dead.

Haley: Then if you wish you were dead . . .

Zario: Then I wouldn't have to worry about nothing.

Haley: Why don't you *shut up* if you wish you were dead and let me talk, why don't you quit talking about me and realise that I love you . . .

Zario: I feel good about you, I don't feel bad about you.

Haley: Oh well, then I *don't* love you and I hate Jack Howard

160

and go *fuck* yourself. Goodbye and don't ever call me. You don't have my fucking number and I didn't give you any fucking numbers. You cannot let Bill Haley say anything and keep his fucking mouth shut. *Now* can I talk?

Haley: And when I'm finished talking, then you can open your mouth. I *do* remember Rex Zario. I *do* remember Philadelphia. I *do* remember Dave Wilson. I know I have a friend named Rex Zario and that's why I called you first.

So you see if you let *me* talk I'll wish you a Merry Christmas . . .

Epilogue

BILL HALEY DIED a broken, insane man. In his last days he was tortured by confusing specters of his past. He knew he had accomplished something great, but he wasn't really sure what it was. He was the product of an essentially rural upbringing and as such was completely unprepared for the show business sophistication he would encounter as a rock & roll star. Critics confounded him, yet he would bravely fight off his jitters to explain his thoughts about rock & roll to interviewers.

At the end, though, the shyness he always suffered from became acute paranoia as the drinking grew worse and hallucination shared the same space with reality. In a remarkable interview with Clem Taylor for a National Public Radio show in the U.S., Haley's oldest son Jack gave a harrowing account of his father's mental condition as of October, 1980, only four months before his death.

'He would talk about his life in the Marine Corps, which he was never in,' said Jack. 'He was never in the service at all. He said he was a deputy sheriff down there in Texas, which he wasn't. I knew he was lying but I never dared say it. I didn't wanna make him mad for fear that I would never hear from him again.'

At the end of his visit, Jack was frightened by his father's behavior. 'He was sitting at the kitchen table with a bottle. I couldn't get him to put the bottle down. He didn't threaten me in any way but he scared me with the way he was talking. He'd talk real loud and holler. I called this Buddy Larimore, captain of the police department, he was the one who came and got me. And he told my father, he said "Bill, you gotta quit the drinking. You're losing the people you love the most." He said "Your wife has left you and went with her family, now your son wants to leave you again." He seemed then that he didn't care.'

Shortly before his death Haley moved out of the house he'd been living in and into the garage, where he barricaded himself against unseen enemies by covering the windows with black spray paint and installing floodlights outside to ward off whoever was out to get him.

Haley's tremendous disorientation was evidenced in brief forays out of his lair. According to a report by Chet Flippo in *Rolling Stone* magazine, a Harlingen police officer said that 'the police would often find him wandering along the country roads, not knowing where he was'.

Barbara Billnitzer, a waitress at Sambo's restaurant in Harlingen, told reporters that Haley came into the place frequently before his death. 'He always seemed real lonely,' she said. 'Sometimes he would walk in and tell us he was Bill Haley and show us his driver's licence. Sometimes he would walk up to different customers and introduce himself. When he'd tell you who he was he'd act like it was a secret.'

Carl Strong was one of the customers Haley introduced himself to. 'He was quite likeable,' said Strong. 'Sometimes he would sit at the counter and look at nothing. Sometimes he'd order a meal and not even eat it. But when Haley did feel like talking he would say "I'm the guy who wrote 'Rock Around the Clock'," then he'd show me his driver's licence. Sometimes he'd sit at the counter and start singing. Then he'd talk to people like he wanted them to figure out who he was without him having to tell them.'

Bill Haley died on February 9, 1981. The cause was officially described as 'natural causes most likely heart attack'. A statement by Harlingen Justice of the Peace Tommy Thompson described the circumstances. 'A friend of his went by to see him and found the house locked and no one answered. He had been dead about six hours because a captain at the police department talked with him about 6:30 this morning.

'He was lying on a bed in a normal fashion as though he were asleep,' stated Thompson. 'He was friendly with me but he was not an outgoing individual. He had problems.'

STATE OF TEXAS — CERTIFICATE OF DEATH

STATE FILE NO

NAME OF DECEASED (Type or print)	(a) First: **William** (b) Middle: **John Clifton** (c) Last: **Haley**	2 SEX **Male**	1 DATE OF DEATH **2/9/81**

3 RACE **White**

4a WAS THE DECEDENT OF SPANISH ORIGIN? **N/A**
4b IF YES, SPECIFY MEXICAN, CUBAN, PUERTO RICAN, ETC. **N/A**

6 DATE OF BIRTH **7/6/1925**

7 AGE (in years last birthday) **55**

5a PLACE OF DEATH — COUNTY **Cameron**

8a NAME OF (If not in hospital, give street address) HOSPITAL OR INSTITUTION **1902 South 1st**

5b CITY OR TOWN (If outside city limits give precinct no) **Harlingen**

10 BIRTHPLACE (State or foreign country) **Michigan**

11 CITIZEN OF WHAT COUNTRY **USA**

12 WAS DECEDENT EVER IN U.S. ARMED FORCES? **No**

9 MARRIED NEVER MARRIED WIDOWED DIVORCED (Specify) **Married**

13 SURVIVING SPOUSE (If wife give maiden name) **Martha Velasco**

15a USUAL OCCUPATION (Give kind of work done during most of working life, even if retired) **Singer**

15b KIND OF BUSINESS OR INDUSTRY **Music**

14 SOCIAL SECURITY NO **186-14-7664**

16a RESIDENCE — STATE **Texas**
16b COUNTY **Cameron**
16c CITY OR TOWN **Harlingen**
16d STREET ADDRESS **1902 South 1st Street**
16e INSIDE CITY LIMITS **yes**

17 FATHER'S NAME **William Haley**

18 MOTHER'S MAIDEN NAME **Manda Green**

19 SIGNATURE OF INFORMANT **Martha Haley**

CAUSE OF DEATH

PART I — IMMEDIATE CAUSE (Enter only one cause per line for (a) (b) (c))
(a) **Natural Causes most likely heart attack**
DUE TO, OR AS A CONSEQUENCE OF:
(b)
DUE TO, OR AS A CONSEQUENCE OF:
(c)

PART II — OTHER SIGNIFICANT CONDITIONS — CONDITIONS CONTRIBUTING TO DEATH BUT NOT RELATED TO CAUSE GIVEN IN PART I (a)

21 AUTOPSY? **No**

22a DESCRIBE HOW INJURY OCCURRED

23a ACC SUICIDE HOM UNDET CAR PENDING INVEST (Specify)

22b DATE OF INJURY (Mo, Day, Yr)
22c HOUR OF INJURY

23b INJURY AT WORK (Specify yes or no)

22d PLACE OF INJURY — At home, farm, street, factory, office building, etc. (Specify)

22e LOCATION STREET OR R F D NO CITY OR TOWN STATE

24a On the basis of examination and/or investigation, in my opinion death occurred at the time, date and place and due to the cause(s) stated (Signature and Title)

24b DATE SIGNED (Mo, Day, Yr) **2/11/81**

24c HOUR OF DEATH **app. 4:00 a.**

24d NAME OF ATTENDING PHYSICIAN (Type or print)

23c PRONOUNCED DEAD (Mo, Day, Year) ON **2/9/81**

23d PRONOUNCED DEAD (Hour) **12:35P.**

25 NAME OF CEMETERY OR CREMATORY **South Texas Crematory**

26 SIGNATURE OF FUNERAL DIRECTOR OR PERSON ACTING AS SUCH

18a BURIAL CREMATION REMOVAL (Specify) **Cremation**

18b LOCATION **Brownsville**

18c DATE **2/12/81**

27a FUNERAL HOME **Kreidler-Ashcraft**
27b LOCATION **Texas**

28 SIGNATURE OF LOCAL REGISTRAR

28a DATE REC'D BY LOCAL REGISTRAR **2/11/81**

Texas Department of Health — BUREAU OF VITAL STATISTICS

Reclusive Rock Star Bill Haley Dies In Harlingen

By SUSAN STOLER
Associated Press Writer

HARLINGEN — Bill Haley, whose hit record "Rock Around the Clock" blared from 1950s jukeboxes and is credited for inspiring the term "Rock N Roll," spent his final years of life seeking a privacy that was continued, even in death, by his widow.

Haley died Monday at this two-story wooden house where he was pronounced dead at 12:35 p.m. He was found alone and lying fully-clothed on a bed.

Justice of the Peace Tommy Thompson said death was from natural causes and said he assumed Haley had suffered a heart attack about six hours earlier. A friend had gone by to visit Haley, Thompson said, and became concerned when he did not answer the door.

The former rock star was 56 according to a July 6, 1925, birthdate on his Texas drivers license. Musicians reference books listed his birthdate as March 1927, making him 53.

The funeral home in charge of arrangements said Monday night that his widow had banned release of any information, including the names of his survivors.

"She doesn't want anything released right now," a funeral home spokesman said.

Haley lived the last five or six years of his life here in semi-reclusion, refusing interviews and even denying his identity to reporters.

One reporter went to his house and was told he had never lived there and was unknown to the house's occupants.

"He tried to keep a low profile," said Harlingen Police Chief Guy Anderson. "I remember when he first moved here and some of the TV people found out and tried to do an interview with him and he refused."

Haley got to know several policemen, who frequently picked him up wandering alone at night and took him home.

"He was friendly with me but he was not an outgoing individual," Thompson said. "He had problems."

A police officer, who asked not to be named, said Haley called him repeatedly last weekend and appeared to be "hallucinating."

"He called me up again and again to talk five or 10 minutes. He just wanted someone to talk to," the officer said.

Haley was born in Highland Park, Mich. His mother was a church organist and his father played banjo. Both encouraged him to learn guitar.

He left home at age 15 to travel with a country band. As an experiment, he played a rhythm and blues tune one night. He changed the name of the seven-piece band to Bill Haley and the Comets.

In 1954, he moved from a small record label to Decca, where his first release was Jimmy DeKnight's "Rock Around the Clock," but it flopped at first. "Shake Rattle and Roll," a remake of a Joe Turner tune, made the top 10 in 1954.

"Rock Around the Clock" became the theme for the movie "Blackboard Jungle" in 1955 and shot Haley's group to further fame. The song returned 20 years later as the movie theme for "American Graffiti" and then the "Happy Days" television series.

Among Haley's other top ten hits were "See You Later, Alligator" 1954, "Dim, Dim The Lights" 1955, and "Crazy, Man, Crazy" 1953.

Haley enjoyed success in Europe, where he lived in the 1960s. He toured in the rock 'n' roll revival of the 1970s, giving a Royal Command Performance for Queen Elizabeth II of Great Britain in 1979. Haley once told an English newspaper he retired briefly when Rudy Pompilli, a close friend and fellow performer, died.

"We (he and Pompilli) had a joke, a promise we made. We used to tell each other, 'If you die first, I'll never play again.' We thought we'd live forever. When he died of cancer I retired. A depression hit me. After working together for 25 years we were like brothers. He was my drinking buddy, the leader of my band," he said in an interview published last year.

Discography

IN ORDER TO avoid duplication as much as possible, EPs or LPs that are simply compilations of previously released singles are not listed.

1948 – *Bill Haley and the Four Aces of Western Swing*

'Four Leaf Clover Blues'/'Too Many Parties, Too Many Pals' *(Cowboy 1700)*
'Candy Kisses'/'Tennessee Border' *(Cowboy 1701)*
'My Palomino and I'/'My Sweet Little Girl From Nevada' *(Cowboy 1701)*

1949 – *Bill Haley and the Four Aces of Western Swing*

'Stand Up and Be Counted'/'Loveless Blues' *(Center)*

1949 – *Bill Haley and the Saddlemen*

'Deal Me A Hand (I Play the Game Anyway)'/'Ten Gallon Stetson (With a Hole In the Crown)' *(Keystone 5101)*

1950 – *Bill Haley and the Saddlemen*

'Susan Van Dusen'/'I'm Not To Blame' *(Keystone 5102)*
'Why Do I Cry Over You'/'I'm Gonna Dry Every Tear With a Kiss' *(Atlantic 727)*

1951 – *Bill Haley and the Saddlemen*

'Rocket 88'/'Tearstains On My Heart' *(Holiday 105)*
'Green Tree Boogie'/'Down Deep In My Heart *(Holiday 108)*
'I'm Crying'/'Pretty Baby' *(Holiday 110)*
'A Year Ago This Christmas'/'Don't Want to Be Alone This Christmas' *(Holiday 111)*

1952 – *Bill Haley and the Saddlemen*

'Jukebox Cannonball'/'Sundown Boogie' *(Holiday 113)*
'Icy Heart'/'Rock the Joint' *(Essex 303)*
'Rocking Chair On the Moon'/'Dance With a Dolly (With a Hole In Her Stocking)' *(Essex 305)*
Bill Haley and His Comets
'Stop Beatin' Round the Mulberry Bush'/'Real Rock Drive' *(Essex 310)*

1953 – *Bill Haley and His Comets*

'Crazy Man, Crazy'/'Watcha Gonna Do' *(Essex 321)*
'Pat-a-Cake'/'Fractured' *(Essex 327)*
'Live It Up'/'Farewell So Long Goodbye' *(Essex 332)*
'I'll Be True'/'Ten Little Indians' *(Essex 340)*
'Straight Jacket'/'Chattanooga Choo-Choo' *(Essex 348)*
'Yes Indeed'/'Real Rock Drive' *(Transworld 718)*

1954

'(We're Gonna) Rock Around the Clock'/'Thirteen Women (And Only One Man In Town)' *(Decca 29124)*
'Shake, Rattle and Roll'/'A.B.C. Boogie' *(Decca 29204)*
'Dim, Dim the Lights (I Want Some Atmosphere)'/'Happy Baby' *(Decca 29317)*

1955

'Mambo Rock'/'Birth of the Boogie' *(Decca 29418)*
'Razzle-Dazzle'/'Two Hound Dogs' *(Decca 29552)*
'Rock-a-Beatin' Boogie'/'Burn That Candle' *(Decca 29713)*
'See You Later, Alligator'/'The Paper Boy (On Main Street, U.S.A.)' *(Decca 29791)*

1956

'The Saints Rock 'N' Roll'/'R-O-C-K' *(Decca 29870)*
'Hot Dog Buddy Buddy'/'Rockin' Through the Rye' *(Decca 29948)*
'Rip It Up'/'Teenager's Mother (Are You Right?)' *(Decca 30028)*
'Rudy's Rock'/'Blue Comet Blues' *(Decca 30085)*
'Don't Knock the Rock'/'Choo Choo Ch' Boogie' *(Decca 30148)*
Rock 'N' Roll Stage Show (LP): 'Calling All Comets', 'Rockin' Through the Rye', 'Rudy's Rock', 'Hook, Line and Sinker', 'A Rocking Little Tune', 'Choo Choo Ch' Boogie', 'Hide and Seek', 'Blue Comet Blues', 'Hey Then, There Now', 'Goofin' Around', 'Hot Dog Buddy Buddy', 'Tonight's the Night' *(Decca 8345)*

1957

'Forty Cups of Coffee'/'Hook, Line and Sinker' *(Decca 30214)*
'(You Hit the Wrong Note) Billy Goat'/'Rockin' Rollin' Rover'
   (Decca 30314)
'The Dipsy Doodle'/'Miss You' *(Decca 30394)*
'Rock the Joint'/'How Many' *(Decca 30461)*
Rockin' the Oldies (LP): 'Miss You', 'The Dipsy Doodle', 'Please
   Don't Talk About Me When I'm Gone', 'You Can't Stop Me From
   Dreaming', 'I'm Gonna Sit Right Down and Write Myself a
   Letter', 'Rock Lomond', 'Is It True What They Say About Dixie?',
   'Carolina In the Morning', 'Ain't Misbehavin' (I'm Savin' My Love
   For You)', 'Moon Over Miami', 'One Sweet Letter From You', '(I'll
   Be With You) In Apple Blossom Time', 'Somebody Else Is Taking
   My Place' *(Decca 8569)*
Rip It Up (EP): 'The Beak "Speaks" ', 'Sway With Me', 'Forty Cups
   of Coffee', 'Rip It Up' *(Decca 2616)*

Note: 'Move It On Over' was also recorded by Haley and the Comets
in 1957 although release information is not included here.

1958

'Mary, Mary Lou'/'It's a Sin' *(Decca 30530)*
'Skinny Minnie'/'Sway With Me' *(Decca 30592)*
'Lean Jean'/'Don't Nobody Move' *(Decca 30681)*
'Chiquita Linda (Un Poquito De Tu Amor)'/'Whoa Mabel' *(Decca
   30741)*
'Corrine, Corrina'/'B.B. Betty' *(Decca 30781)*
Bill Haley Chicks (LP): 'Whoa Mabel', 'Ida, Sweet As Apple Cider',
   'Eloise', 'Dinah', 'Skinny Minnie', 'Mary, Mary Lou', 'Sweet Sue,
   Just You', 'B.B. Betty', 'Charmaine', 'Corrine, Corrina', 'Marie',
   'Lean Jean' *(DL 8821)*
Rockin' Around the World (LP): 'Pretty Alouette', 'Piccadilly Rock',
   'Rockin' Rolling Schnitzelbank', 'Vive la Rock & Roll', 'Come
   Rock With Me', 'Wooden Shoe Rock', 'Rock a Hula', 'Oriental
   Rock', 'Rockin' Matilda', 'El Rocko', 'Rocking Rita', 'Jamaica
   D.J.' *(Decca DL8692)*

Note: Haley and the Comets also recorded 'The Walking Beat' in
1958.

1959

'Charmaine'/'I Got a Woman' *(Decca 30844)*
'(Now and Then There's) a Fool Such As I'/'Where'd You Go Last
   Night?' *(Decca 30873)*

'Caldonia'/'Shaky' *(Decca 30926)*

'Ooh! Look-a-There, Ain't She Pretty?'/'Joey's Song' *(Decca 30956)*

Strictly Instrumental (LP): 'Joey's Song', 'Music! Music! Music!',
'Mack the Knife', 'In a Little Spanish Town', 'Two Shadows',
'Shaky', 'Strictly Instrumental', 'Skokiaan (South Africa song)',
'Puerto Rican Peddler', 'Drowsy Waters', 'Chiquita Linda (Un
Poquito De Tu Amor)', 'The Catwalk' *(DL 8964)*

Note: Haley and the Comets also recorded 'The Dragon Rock', 'ABC
Rock', 'Be By Me' and '(Thanks For The) Summer Souvenir' in 1959.

1960

'Candy Kisses'/'Tamiami' *(Warner Bros. 5145)*

'Chick Safari'/'Hawk' *(Warner Bros. 5154)*

'So Right Tonight'/'Let the Good Times Roll, Creole' *(Warner Bros.
5171)*

'Flip, Flop, and Fly'/'Honky Tonky' *(Warner Bros. 5228)*

Haley's Jukebox (LP): 'Singing the Blues', 'Candy Kisses', 'No Letter
Today', 'This Is the Thanks I Get', 'Bouquet of Roses', 'There's a
New Moon Over My Shoulder', 'Cold, Cold Heart', 'The Wild Side
of Life', 'Any Time', 'Afraid', 'I Don't Hurt Anymore', 'Detour'
(Warner Bros. W 1391)

1961

'The Spanish Twist'/'My Kind of Woman' *(Gone 5111)*

'Riviera'/'War Paint' *(Gone 5116)*

'Florida Twist'/'Negra Consentida' *(Orfeon 1047)*

1962

'Pure De Papas'/'Anoche' *(Orfeon 1195)*

Twistin' Knights At the Round Table (Recorded Live) (LP): 'Lullaby
of Birdland Twist', 'Twist Marie', 'One-Two-Three Twist', 'Down
By the Riverside Twist', 'Queen of the Twisters', 'Caravan Twist',
'I Want a Little Girl', 'Whistlin' and Walkin' Twist', 'Florida
Twist', 'Eight More Miles to Louisville' *(Roulette R 25174)*

1963

'Tenor Man'/'Up Goes My Love' *(Newtown 5013)*

'Midnight In Washington'/'White Parakeet' *(Newtown 5014)*

'Dance Around the Clock'/'What Can I Say After I Say I'm Sorry'
(Newtown 5024)

'Tandy'/'You Call Everybody Darling' *(Newtown 5025)*

1964

'The Green Door'/'Yeah, She's Evil!' *(Decca 31650)*

1965

'Burn That Candle'/'Stop, Look and Listen' *(Apt 25081)*
'Haley A Go Go'/'Tongue Tied Tony' *(Apt 25087)*

Note: In the 1960s Haley recorded extensively in Mexico for Orfeon Records. Three albums' worth of that material are currently available.

Bill Haley Y Sus Cometas (LP): 'Ahi Nos Vemos Cocodrilo', 'Boogie A.B.C.', 'Nueva Orleans', 'Nocturno De Harlem', 'Let's Twist Again', 'Florida Twist', 'Silbando Y Caminando', 'Tren Nocturno', 'Negra Consentida', 'Rip It Up' *(Orfeon 1037)*

Discos Del Millon De Rock & Roll And Twist (LP): 'Rock Around the Clock', 'La Marcha De Los Santos', 'Rip It Up', 'Razzle Dazzle', 'Hay Nos Vemos Cocodrilo', 'Florida Twist', 'Pure De Papas', 'La Tierra De Las Mil Danzas', 'Mas Twist', 'El Blues De Los Cometas' *(Orfeon 2084)*

Al Compas Del Reloj (LP): 'Al Compas Del Reloj', 'Baja California Sun', 'Cerca Del Mar', 'Comet Boogie', 'El Madison', 'El Expreso', 'Jarrito Twist', 'Mish Mashed', 'No Te Puedes Sentar', 'Puerta Verde' *(Orfeon 9064)*

1968

Biggest Hits (LP): 'Rock Around the Clock', 'Skinny Minnie', 'Ling-Ting-Tong', 'Rock the Joint', 'Rock-a-Beatin' Boogie', 'See You Later Alligator', 'Flip Flop and Fly', 'The Saints Rock and Roll', 'Shake, Rattle & Roll' *(Sonet GP-9945)*

1969

'That's How I Got To Memphis', 'Ain't Love Funny, Ha Ha Ha' *(United Artists 50483)*

Bill Haley On Stage (LP): 'Shake Rattle and Roll', 'Skinny Minnie', 'Rip It Up', 'Rudy's Rock', 'Lucille', 'Whole Lotta Shakin' Goin' On', 'See You Later Alligator', 'Caravan', 'Kansas City', 'What'd I Say', 'Rock Around the Clock', 'Razzle Dazzle', 'Cryin' Time', 'Yakety Sax', 'Jenny, Jenny', 'Johnny B. Goode', 'The Saints Rock and Roll', 'Rock-A-Beatin' Boogie', 'Malaguena', 'Guitar Boogie', 'New Orleans', 'Rock the Joint' *(Sonet GPD-9989)*

1970

'Rock Around the Clock'/'Framed' *(Kama Sutra 508)*

Bill Haley's Scrapbook (LP): 'Rock the Joint', 'Rock-a-Beatin'
Boogie', 'Rip It Up', 'Razzle Dazzle', 'Framed', 'Rock Around the
Clock', 'Crazy Man, Crazy', 'When the Saints Go Marching In',
'Shake Rattle and Roll', 'Skinny Minnie', 'Rudy's Rock', 'See You
Later Alligator' *(Kama Sutra BSBS 20114)*

1971

Rock Around the Country (LP): 'Me and Bobby McGee', 'How
Many', 'Who'll Stop the Rain', 'Pink Eyed Pussycat', 'Travelin'
Band', 'No Letter Today', 'Dance Around the Clock', 'Games
People Play', 'A Little Piece at a Time', 'I Wouldn't Have Missed
It For the World', 'Bony Maronie', 'There's a New Moon Over My
Shoulder' *(Sonet GP-10040)*

1973 ⁝

Just Rock and Roll Music (LP): 'I'm Walkin' ', 'High Heel Sneakers',
'Blue Suede Shoes', 'Tossin' and Turnin' ', 'Flip, Flop & Fly',
-'Whole Lotta Shakin' Goin' On', 'C.C. Rider', 'Lawdy Miss
Clawdy', 'Bring It On Home To Me', 'Personality', 'Crazy Man,
Crazy', 'Rock & Roll Music' *(Sonet SNTF 645)*

1976

R-O-C-K (LP): 'Ooh! Look-a-There, Ain't She Pretty', 'Dim, Dim
the Lights', 'Burn That Candle', 'I Got a Woman', 'R-O-C-K',
'Farewell, So Long, Good-Bye', 'A.B.C. Boogie', 'Dance With a
Dolly', 'I'll Be True To You', 'Mohair Sam' *(Sonet SNTF-710)*

1979

Everyone Can Rock and Roll (LP): 'Hail, Hail Rock and Roll', 'Jim
Dandy', 'That's How I Got To Memphis', 'Juke Box Cannonball',
'Let the Good Times Roll Again', 'God Bless Rock and Roll',
'Everyone Can Rock and Roll', 'The Battle of New Orleans', 'I
Need the Music', 'Heartaches By the Number', 'Tweedle Dee', 'So
Right Tonight' *(Sonet SNTF 808)*

Index

'ABC Boogie', 50, 126, 132
'Ain't misbehavin' ', 105
American Society of Composers,
  Authors & Publishers (ASCAP),
  24
Anthony, John, 30, 41
'Apple Blossom Time', 105
Atlantic Records, 29
Autry, Gene, 17, 24

Barnard, Barney, 25
'Beak Speaks, The', 105
Beatles, 8, 79, 138
Beecher, Frank, 9, 59, 60, 64, 65,
  69, 71, 72, 80, 104, 105, 108, 112,
  115, 132, 133
'Behind the Eight Ball', 27
Berliner Zeitung, 154
Berry, Chuck, 46, 71, 111
Bild, 153
Bill Haley's Juke Box, 129
'Billy Goat', 104
Blackboard Jungle, 7, 57–58, 130
'Blue Comet Blues', 71
Boone, Pat, 56, 105
Braceland, Francis J, 72
Branner, Arthur, 121
Brenston, Jackie, 32, 34
British Tour (1956), 86–103
Britt, Elton, 21
Broadcast Music Industry (BMI),
  25
Broomall, Vince 'Catfish', 90, 116
Burch, Wolfgang, 153

'Caldonia', 127

Calhoun, Charles, 51
'Calling All Comets', 71, 79
'Candy Kisses', 25, 129
'Carolina In the Morning', 105
Carter, Asa, 73
'Catwalk, The', 126
Cedrone, Danny, 34, 40, 42, 44, 47,
  59, 60
Center Records, 26, 29
Charters, Sam, 140, 144, 145, 146,
  147, 150, 151
'Choo Choo Ch' Boogie', 71
Clark, Dick, 35, 111
Columbia Records, 112
Comets, 12, 14, 58, 63; break-up,
  133; British Tour, 86–103;
  musical approach, 7–8; musical
  peak, 70–72; name, 42;
  Pompilli's influence on, 69,
  70–71; and rock & roll violence,
  75–76, 86–87, 119–123; stage
  act, 63, 98; world tour, 81–82
Commodore Records, 46
Constantine, Al, 25
Cook, Shorty, 21
Coral Records, 67
Cornell, Lloyd, 22
'Covered Wagon Rolled Right
  Along, The', 27
Cowboy Records, 24, 29
'Crazy Man, Crazy', 42, 43, 44, 46,
  62, 69, 113, 147
Crickets, 8, 67
'Crossover' music, 21–2, 25, 27, 35
Crowe, Dorothy, 20, 23, 30, 38–9,
  155

Cupchack, Barbara Joan, 38, 85, 90, 92, 93, 102–103, 134

Daily Mirror, 86–100, 138
Daily Sketch, 94, 96, 99, 100
Daily Telegraph, 101
'Dance With a Dolly', 40–41, 42
Danny and the Juniors, 111
Decca Records, 46, 49, 50, 52, 58, 65, 67, 81, 107, 125, 128
'Deep Down In My Heart', 35
Denton, Kenny, 153
'Dinah', 125
'Dipsy Doodle', 105
Don't Knock the Rock, 78–79, 83, 103
'Down By the Riverside Twist', 132
Downhomers, 21, 22
'Dragon Rock', 126

Essex Records, 29, 33, 35, 45, 46
Evening Standard, 153
Everyone Can Rock and Roll, 153

'Farewell, So Long, Goodbye', 150
Feddis, Jim, 112–113, 114–115, 116–117, 144
Field, Irving, 78, 81
Ferguson, Lord Jim, 30, 38, 41, 58, 66, 81, 90, 96, 109, 114, 115, 116, 119, 122, 123–124, 128, 130
'Florida Twist', 131
'Foolish Questions', 24
Ford, Glenn, 57
Four Aces of Western Swing, 25, 26
'Four Leaf Clover Blues', 22, 25
Freed, Alan, 43, 74, 78, 111
Freedman, Max, 44

Gabler, Milt, 46–47, 48, 49, 50, 51, 52, 53, 70, 80, 105, 106, 108, 112, 114, 125, 134, 136, 156
Gillespie, Dizzy, 37
'Go Man Go Get Gone', 156
'Goofin' Around', 71
Gordon, Lee, 84
Grade, Lew, 100

Grande, John, 26, 27, 33, 47, 53, 59, 91, 134
Greco, Buddy, 59
'Green Door', 136
'Greentree Boogie', 35
Guesack, Billy, 47, 70

Haley, Bill,
ambition, 20, 23, 26; birth, 15; childhood, 15–19; children, 25, 29, 39, 58, 80–81, 144; death, 162–163; drink and drugs, 88, 144; fans, 93, 94, 95, 96, 102; first recordings, 25; image, 41–42, 43, 88–89; marriage, 23, 38, 80, 113, 133, 134; Melody Manor, 80, 81, 106, 134; money, 108–109, 110, 112, 113, 114, 128; musical approach, 7, 36, 53, 65; musical abilities, 55; parents, 15, 17, 18, 58, 80; 'Rock Around the Clock', recording of, 46–50; rock & roll, champion of, 8, 153; shyness, 18, 21, 23, 83, 117; yodelling, 21, 27–28
Haley, Jack, 162–163
'Happy Baby', 59, 109
Happy Days, 13
'Has Anybody Seen My Gal', 19
Hawkins, Hankshaw, 19
Hier Bin Ich, Hier Bliebe Ich (Here I Am, Here I Stay), 121
'Hey Then, There Now,' 71
'Hide and Seek', 71
Holiday Records, 33, 35
Holly, Buddy, 8, 67–68, 111
'Hook, Line and Sinker', 71
'Hot Dog Buddy Buddy', 71, 76, 77, 106
Howard, Jack, 20, 24, 25, 27, 30, 32, 36, 41, 127, 134, 156
'How Many', 107
'Hucklebuck, The', 71

'Icy Heart', 36, 37
'Ida, Sweet As Apple Cider', 125

'I Got a Woman', 127, 150
'I'm Gonna Dry Every Tear With a Kiss', 29
Ink Spots, 51, 52, 65
'Is It True What They Say About Dixie?', 105

Jodimars, 59, 63, 109
'Joey's Song', 125
Jones, Ralph, 9, 45, 59, 62, 64, 70, 71, 72, 78, 82, 88, 99, 115, 122, 125–126, 129, 132, 145
Jordon, Louis, 51, 52, 53, 71, 127
Joyce, Jolly, 72, 90, 100, 109, 114, 126, 144, 146
'Jukebox Cannonball', 35, 153
Just Rock and Roll Music, 144, 146

Katzman, Sam, 72
Keefer, Rusty, 26, 108
'Keep Smiling', 20
King, Tex, 25, 26

'Lean Jean', 111, 126
Lee, Alvin, 65
Lewis, Jerry Lee, 68, 144
Little Richard, 79
'Long Tall Sally', 79, 88
'Loveless Blues', 26
Lytle, Marshall, 47, 58

'Mack the Knife', 128
Malynn, Patrick, 138, 146, 151, 154
'Mambo Rock', 34
Manchester Guardian, 98, 100–101
Manfred Mann, 137
'Marie', 124
Martieri, Ralph, 61–62
Mason, Bob, 22
Melody Maker, 96, 97, 98
Miller, Dave, 32, 33, 34, 35, 36, 43, 45, 46, 156
Miller, Mitch, 74
'Miss You', 104
'Mohair Sam', 151
'Moon Over Miami', 105
'Move It On Over', 106
'Music, Music, Music', 128

'My Daddy Rock me With a Steady Roll', 50
Myers, James E, 9, 29–30, 35, 44, 45, 46–47, 48, 50, 57, 58, 108–109, 156
'My Mom Heard Me Crying', 27
'My Sweet Little Girl From Nevada', 25

Observer, 97, 98, 99, 101
'One Sweet Letter From You', 105
'Ooh Look-a-There Ain't She Pretty', 127, 150
Orfeon Records, 131

Palda Records, 32
Park, Lee (Cousin Lee), 19, 20, 25
Parker, Colonel Tom, 66, 67
'Pat-a-Cake', 44
Phillips, Sam, 32, 34
Pignatore, Frank, 109
Platters, 72, 82
'Please Don't Talk About Me When I'm Gone', 105
Pompilli, Al, 126
Pompilli, Rudy, 12–14, 59, 61, 62, 69, 70–71, 72, 105, 111, 131, 135, 143, 145, 148–149, 150, 152
Presley, Elvis, 7, 8, 34, 44, 56, 66, 67, 77, 86, 87, 105, 111, 115, 123, 125, 130, 152
'Pure De Papas', 131
Pythian Temple Studio, 47, 53, 104, 105, 126

'Razzle Dazzle', 97, 132
Reichner, Bix, 35, 42, 43
Reno Browne and her Buckeroos, 25
Rex, Al, 9, 26, 27, 29, 30, 33, 36, 38, 40, 41, 43, 59, 63, 64, 71, 83, 88, 95, 116, 126
Richards, Dick, 58, 62
'Rip It Up', 79, 132
Roberts, Kenny, 9–10, 21
R.O.C.K., 150
'R.O.C.K.', 69
'Rock-a-Beatin'-Boogie', 41, 43, 69

173

'Rock Around the Clock', 7, 9, 14, 44–45, 46, 47, 48, 49, 50, 57, 58, 63, 65–66, 99, 108, 129, 132, 139, 142
Rock Around the Clock (film), 70, 72, 86, 109
Rock Around the Country, 142, 150
'Rocket 88', 32, 33, 35, 36, 111
'Rock Lomond', 105
'Rock the Joint', 33, 36, 38, 40, 43, 63, 106
'Rockin' Little Tune', 72
'Rockin' Rollin' Rover', 105
'Rockin' Through the Rye', 72
'Rocking Chair On the Moon', 40
Rolling Stone, 163
Rolling Stones, 34
Rose, Billy, 74
'Rovin' Eyes', 27
'Rudy's Rock', 62, 70, 97

Saddlemen, 26, 27–31, 32, 33, 34, 35, 38, 40, 42, 63, 71, 106, 107
'Saints Rock and Roll', 13, 69
Saperstein, Abe, 115
'See You Later Alligator', 69–70, 132
'Shake, Rattle and Roll', 50, 52, 118
'Shaky', 127
Shore, Dinah, 81
Sinatra, Frank, 51, 84
'Skinny Minnie', 111–112, 134
'Slapback' bass, 36, 47, 51
Snow, Hank, 24, 66
'Somebody Else Is Taking My Place', 106
Sonet Records, 140, 147
Spigot Cafe, 29–30
'Stand Up and Be Counted', 26
Steele, Tommy, 86
Stoner, Rob, 48
'Stop Beating Around the Mulberry Bush', 42
Sun Records, 34
Sunset Records, 127
'Sway With Me', 111

'Tamiamia', 129
'Tearstains On My Heart', 35
'Teenager's Mother', 77, 100
'Tennessee Border', 25
Terry, Ken, 43, 66, 137
'That's How I Got to Memphis', 140
'There's a Fool Such As I', 127
'Thirteen Women', 47
Times, The, 94, 95, 97, 98, 99, 100
Tinker, Dean, 62
'Tonight's the Night', 71
'Too Many Parties, Too Many Pals', 25
Turner, Joe, 51, 69, 82, 127, 132
'Tutti Frutti', 79
Twistin' Knights At the Round Table, 133

Valente, Katerina, 21
Velascao, Martha, 133. 134, 144, 151

'Walking Beat, The', 111
Warner Brothers Records, 128, 131
Weinberg, S Kirson, 73–74
'When the Saints Go Marching In', 13
Whitcomb, Noel, 89–90, 91
'Why Do I Cry Over You?', 29
Williamson, Billy, 26, 27, 34, 40, 47, 53, 59, 63, 64, 71, 91, 97
Willis, Bob & His Texas Playboys, 27
Wilson, Meredith, 74
'Within This Broken Heart of Mine', 27
'Wreck On the Highway', 27

'Yes, She's Evil', 136
'Yodeller's Lullaby', 27
'Yodel Your Blues Away', 26, 36
'You Can't Stop Me From Dreaming', 105
'You Made Me Love You', 97

Zario, Rex, 156–161